Why do the right words always come out of the wrong mouth?

Other Cathy® Books From Andrews and McMeel

A hand to hold, an opinion to reject
Thin thighs in thirty years
Wake me up when I'm a size 5
Men should come with instruction booklets
A mouthful of breath mints and no one to kiss
Another Saturday night of wild and reckless abandon

Why do the right words always come out of the wrong mouth?

by Cathy Guisewite

Andrews and McMeel
A Universal Press Syndicate Company
Kansas City • New York

 For information write Andrews and McMeel, a Universal Press Syndicate Company, 4900 Main Street, Kansas City, Missouri 64112.

ISBN: 0-8362-1808-6
Library of Congress Catalog Card Number: 88-71102

I WAS SO GLAD YOU COULD COME OUT TONIGHT, CATHY!
HOW CAN I TELL HIM I DON'T WANT TO SEE HIM ANYMORE?

I'VE BEEN PLANNING THIS EVENING ALL WEEK!
HE'S PERFECTLY NICE. I JUST DON'T LIKE HIM.

I CLEANED MY WHOLE APARTMENT IN CASE WE STOPPED BACK HERE!
WHAT CAN I SAY?? WHAT GROUNDS DO I HAVE??

WOULD YOU LIKE ANYTHING?
DO SOMETHING OBNOXIOUS.

OF COURSE, I'D HATE TO PRESSURE YOU, CATHY, BUT ANOTHER WOMAN IS MAKING AN OFFER ON THAT CONDO YOU LIKED SO MUCH....
YOU HAVE AN-OTHER BUYER?!
CATHY

...WELL. ANOTH-ER BROKER SHOWED ME A BETTER UNIT FOR LESS MONEY.
YOU HAVE ANOTHER BROKER?? ...WELL. MY BUYER IS PAYING CASH!
CATHY

HAH! MY BROKER HAS 7 CONDOS IN MY PRICE RANGE AND DROPPED HER COMMISSION!
HAH! HAH! ONE MO-MENT, PLEASE.

HER FICTITIOUS OTHER BROKER IS BEATING OUT MY FICTI-TIOUS OTHER BUYER.
NEW LISTINGS!
LIVING SPACE SPECIALIST
Guisewite

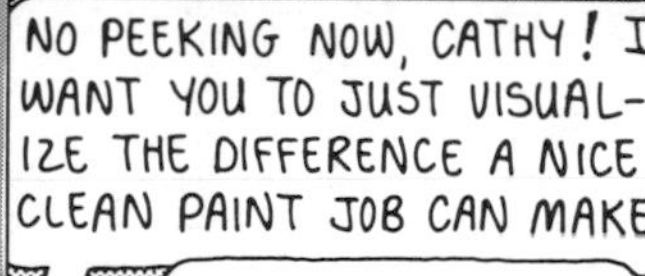
NO PEEKING NOW, CATHY! I WANT YOU TO JUST VISUAL-IZE THE DIFFERENCE A NICE CLEAN PAINT JOB CAN MAKE.

I'M VISUALIZING...
NEW LISTINGS

VISUALIZE NEW CARPETS...
I'M VISUALIZING...
VISUALIZE NEW LIGHTS...
I'M VISUALIZING...
VISUALIZE MINOR REPAIRS...

I'M VISUALIZING! I'M VISUALIZING! YES!!
OK, NOW SLOWLY OPEN YOUR EYES AND TAKE A LOOK AT YOUR DREAM HOUSE!!
NEW LISTINGS

AACK! BLEAH! ICK ACK!!!
YOU'RE VERBALIZING.
Guisewite

$150,000. FOR THIS?! DON'T MAKE ME LAUGH!
IRVING, YOU HAVEN'T BEEN LOOKING WITH ME. YOU DON'T KNOW WHAT THINGS COST.

I WOULDN'T PAY HALF THAT FOR THIS PEA-NUT SHELL!
I'VE LOOKED AT 36 HOMES. I THINK I HAVE A BETTER GRASP OF THE MARKET THAN YOU DO.

YOU'VE BEEN BRAIN-WASHED!
FINE. IGNORE ME. YOU GO AROUND WITH MY AGENT TO THE SAME 36 PLACES I'VE SEEN AND WE'LL SEE WHAT YOU SAY THEN!

MABEL!
BREAK UP.
Guisewite

I THOUGHT THIS WAS A GOOD TIME TO BUY A HOUSE.
NO. IT'S ONLY A GOOD TIME TO BUY A HOUSE WHEN YOU'RE TRYING TO SELL A HOUSE.
NEW LISTING
LIVING SPACE SPECIALIST

SO THIS IS A GOOD TIME TO SELL A HOUSE?
NO: IF YOU WERE TRYING TO SELL A HOUSE, IT WOULD INSTANTLY TURN INTO A GOOD TIME TO BUY A HOUSE.

THE SECOND I GET A CLIENT IT TURNS INTO A GOOD TIME TO DO THE EXACT OPPOSITE OF WHAT SHE WANTS... BUYER'S MARKET... POOF!...SELLER'S MARKET... POOF!...I TRY TO HANG ON FOR MY PEOPLE BUT I'M JUST ONE LITTLE AGENT...

...WAIT.. I'LL GET YOU A TISSUE...
I'VE GIVEN UP ON THE BROKER'S CREDO AND AM GOING FOR THE PITY SALE.
NEW LISTING
LIVING SPACE SPECIALIST
Guisewite

I'VE SHOWN HER 42 PERFECT HOMES.
SHE'S DRAGGED ME TO 42 OVERPRICED DUMPS.
FOR SALE

I'VE FOUND EVERY FEATURE SHE ASKED FOR.
SHE DOESN'T HAVE A CLUE WHAT I WANT.
FOR SALE

I'VE GUIDED, CAJOLED AND FLATTERED, AND NOW I'M GOING TO MAKE MY SALE!!
I'VE PUSHED MY PATIENCE AND MONEY TO THE LIMIT AND I WANT SATISFACTION!!
FOR SALE

THE BROKER AND THE BUYER SIMULTANEOUSLY MOVE IN FOR THE KILL.
Guisewite

ATTENTION ALL EMPLOYEES: CATHY HAS ASKED ME TO ANNOUNCE THAT SHE WILL NO LONGER TOLERATE DISCUSSIONS ABOUT THE FAT FARM OR HER LOVE LIFE DURING BUSINESS HOURS... AS SHE HAS APPARENTLY FOUND A NEW OBSESSION IN REAL ESTATE.
PRODUCT TESTING INC

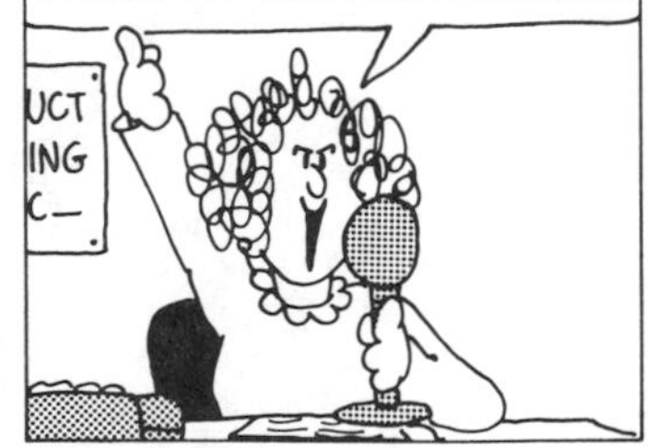
ALL THOSE WISHING TO OFFER THEIR UNSOLICITED OPINIONS ON WHY SHE'S BUYING THE WRONG HOME AT THE WRONG PRICE FROM THE WRONG AGENT PLEASE BARGE INTO HER OFFICE AT YOUR CONVENIENCE.

THINK OF ME AS THE GLUE THAT HOLDS THIS COMPANY TOGETHER.
CATHY
IN
Guisewite

THE CONDO IS PERFECT FOR YOU, AND YOU LOVED IT...
I DON'T KNOW...
THE 23 FRIENDS AND RELATIVES YOU MADE ME SHOW IT TO LOVED IT...
I JUST DON'T KNOW...
NEW HOMES

I HAVE BUYERS COMING WITH A DEPOSIT CHECK IN FIVE MINUTES...
IT'S SUCH A BIG DECISION... I CAN'T THINK ... I CAN'T DECIDE... I JUST DON'T KNOW....

THERE'S ONLY ONE THING WORSE THAN NOT GETTING THE HOME YOU LOVE, CATHY...
I'LL TAKE IT!
SOLD!
AACK!!

GETTING IT.

OUR DAUGHTER HAS BOUGHT A CONDOMINIUM! I CAN'T BELIEVE IT!
I KNOW... REMEMBER GETTING OUR FIRST LITTLE PLACE?

OH, YES! NOTHING IN LIFE COMPARES WITH THE FEELING OF BUYING YOUR FIRST HOME!

WAAAH!! I HATE IT! I BLEW IT! I WANT OUT! I'M NOT READY! I GOT THE WRONG ONE! AAGH I'VE RUINED MY LIFE!!!

SHE LOOKS JUST LIKE YOU DID.

I WANT TO RETURN THE CONDOMINIUM I BOUGHT, MOM.
YOU'RE JUST IN SHOCK AT HAVING MADE A BIG DECISION, CATHY.

LIFE GIVES US SO MANY SPECIAL MOMENTS....EACH ONE A STEPPINGSTONE TO THE NEXT.

IN TIMES LIKE THIS YOU NEED TO DIG INTO YOUR TREASURE CHEST OF EXPERIENCES AND REMEMBER HOW EASILY ANXIETIES WERE OVERCOME IN THE PAST!!

...MY DAUGHTER WANTS TO RETURN THE CONDOMINIUM SHE BOUGHT.

YOU'LL LOVE YOUR NEW CONDO ONCE YOU GET USED TO THE IDEA, CATHY.
NO. IT WAS A MISTAKE. I'M NOT READY. I'M TOO YOUNG.
REALTY
NEW LISTINGS

I WANT OUT. GET ME OUT. I NEED MORE TIME. IT'S A BLUNDER. A BAD DREAM. I WAS TOO IMPULSIVE, TOO CRAZED. IT'S OFF. IT'S OVER. I CAN'T GO THROUGH WITH IT.

I WANT THE OTHER ONE. ANY ONE! ANY ONE BUT THE ONE I PICKED! BAD VIBES! NO DEAL! START OVER! PRETEND YOU NEVER SAW ME AND I'LL START OVER JUST GET ME OUT OF HERE I'M STRANGLING I'M SUFFOCATING!!!

FRIEND OF THE BRIDE OR FRIEND OF THE CONDOMINIUM?
REALTY
Guisewite

I'M GOING TO GET OUT OF MY CONDOMINIUM DEAL ONCE AND FOR ALL!
GO FOR IT!
RECEPTION

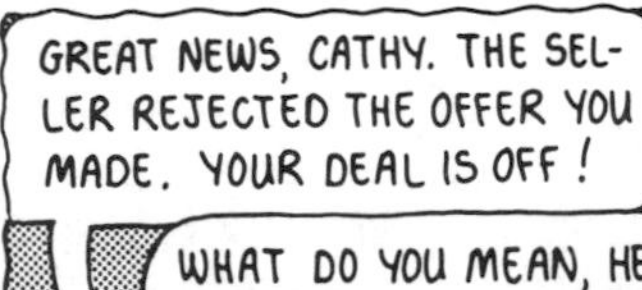
GREAT NEWS, CATHY. THE SELLER REJECTED THE OFFER YOU MADE. YOUR DEAL IS OFF!

WHAT DO YOU MEAN, HE REJECTED MY OFFER??
RIP!

SOMEONE ELSE OFFERED MORE.
I CAN OFFER MORE!
$3,000 MORE.
I'LL MATCH THEIR $3,000 AND ADD $1,000! I MUST HAVE THAT CONDOMINIUM!

WELL, THAT MUST BE A LOAD OFF YOUR MIND!
I HAVE TO LEAVE THE COUNTRY, CHARLENE.
Guisewite

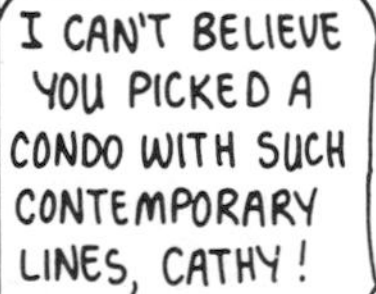

I CAN'T BELIEVE YOU PICKED A CONDO WITH SUCH CONTEMPORARY LINES, CATHY!
THE OLDER STYLES WERE TOO PREDICTABLE, ANDREA.

I WANTED A HOME THAT SAYS I'M SOPHISTICATED... I'M SURPRISING! OPEN AND APPEALING, YES... BUT WITH SOME DAZZLE AND ALLURE!

I WANT MY HOME TO SAY, "HERE I AM, WORLD! TRY AND CATCH ME!" HA, HA!!
THIS IS GOING TO BE EXCITING!

I KNOW... I'M TRYING TO ACCOMPLISH WITH A $100,000 CONDO WHAT I USED TO ACCOMPLISH WITH A $15 BOTTLE OF COLOGNE.
Guisewite

I WANT A MAN WHO'S MORE SPON-TANEOUS WITH ME THAN IRVING IS.
DID YOU TELL IRVING THAT?

NO... I WANT SOMEONE WHO'S COZIER SOMETIMES.
DID YOU MENTION THAT TO IRVING?
NO... I WANT SOMEONE WHO'LL TALK ABOUT PROBLEMS WITH ME.
DID YOU MENTION THAT?

NO.
CATHY, HOW DO YOU EXPECT A MAN TO BE EVERYTHING YOU WANT IF YOU DON'T GIVE HIM A HINT??

I WANT SOMEONE WHO'S A BETTER GUESSER.
Guisewite

I SPEND AN HOUR DOING MY MAKEUP AT HOME, AND IN THE 20 MINUTES IT TAKES ME TO DRIVE TO THE OFFICE IT JUST DISAPPEARS.

ME TOO. IT LOOKS AS IF I DIDN'T EVEN PUT ANY ON.
WHERE DOES IT GO? IT'S NOT ON MY FACE... IT'S NOT ON MY CLOTHES...

I DON'T KNOW, CATHY. IT JUST VANISHES INTO THE AIR.

IT ISN'T SMOG. IT'S EYESHADOW!!!

DRUGS ARE OUT. TOTALLY PASSÉ.... OUR COLOGNE IS CALLED "OPIUM."

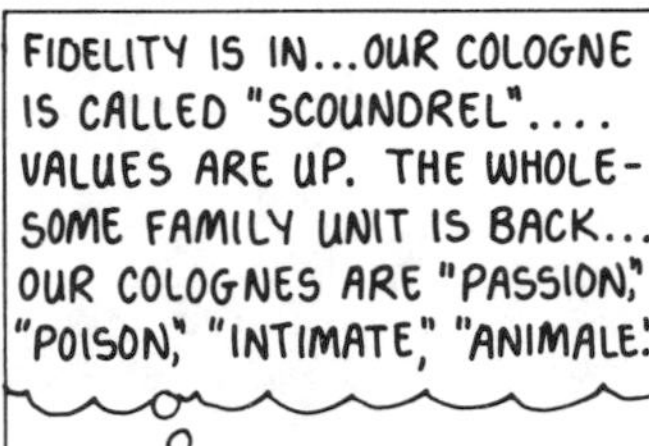
FIDELITY IS IN...OUR COLOGNE IS CALLED "SCOUNDREL".... VALUES ARE UP. THE WHOLE-SOME FAMILY UNIT IS BACK... OUR COLOGNES ARE "PASSION," "POISON," "INTIMATE," "ANIMALE."

OPIUM

THE ESSENCE OF LIFE IN 1987:
OPIUM

AN AIR OF SELF-RIGHTEOUSNESS UNDER A CLOUD OF "OBSESSION."
OPIUM

HOW'S IT GOING, CHARLENE?
"RECKLESS LOVE"..."HEARTS AFLAME"...
CHARLENE

"CAPTIVE EMBRACE"... "BITTERSWEET ECSTASY"... "PASSIONATE VENGEANCE"... "SOAR AND SURRENDER"... "WILD CONQUEST"... "PRISONER OF DESIRE"... "FORBIDDEN CARESS"...

...ABOUT AVERAGE, I'D SAY.

73 SUMMER ROMANCES AND NO DATE.

SORRY, CATHY. MR. FAIRFAX IS ON VACATION.
THIS IS TOP PRIORITY. I'M SURE HE LEFT A PHONE NUMBER FOR ME.
CATHY

OH, YES. HE LEFT SEVERAL.
CATHY

HOWEVER, HE HAS AN ANSWERING MACHINE ON BOTH LINES OF HIS HOME AND BOAT PHONES... HE TURNED OFF HIS CAR PHONE, UNPLUGGED HIS POOL PHONE, TOOK THE BATTERIES OUT OF HIS BEEPER, AND INSTRUCTED ALL HOTEL OPERATORS TO GIVE A CONSTANT BUSY SIGNAL FOR HIS ROOM.

IT ISN'T WHERE WE GO IN LIFE ANYMORE...IT'S HOW MANY WAYS WE CAN'T BE REACHED.
CATHY
Guisewite

DID YOU HAVE YOUR BIG TALK WITH FRANKIE, CHARLENE?
NO. HOW DID YOU DO WITH IRVING?

ZILCH. HE JUST SOUNDED TOO DISTANT TO BRING ANYTHING UP.
FRANKIE SEEMED TOTALLY IN THE DARK. IT WOULD HAVE BEEN POINTLESS TO PRESS THE ISSUE.

SOMETIMES I WONDER HOW MUCH WE'VE BEEN TRAINED BY THE MACHINES IN OUR LIVES.
YEAH...

I NEVER START TALKING UNTIL I HEAR THE TONE.
I DON'T PUSH ANY BUTTONS UNTIL I SEE A LITTLE LIGHT GO ON.
Guisewite

IS IRVING THREATENED THAT YOU HAVE A CONDOMINIUM IN ESCROW, CATHY?
THREATENED? DON'T BE RIDICULOUS, MOM!

YOU HAVEN'T SEEN HIM MUCH LATELY.
I'VE BEEN BUSY... HE'S BEEN BUSY... HE KNOWS I NEED TIME TO ADJUST TO THIS BRAVE STEP.

HE'S GIVING ME SPACE TO DISCOVER WHO I AM WITHOUT COMPLICATING THINGS WITH HIS PRESENCE... HE'S DEMONSTRATING HIS LOVE BY TRYING TO STAY AWAY... HE RESPECTS MY ACHIEVEMENTS TOO MUCH TO INTRUDE ON THIS INTENSELY PERSONAL TIME...

YOU'RE TREADING WATER, DEAR.
I'M BREATHING, AREN'T I?
Guisewite

YOU SEEM SO DETACHED, IRVING. IS EVERYTHING OK?
OK? YEAH, SURE, CATHY...

WE WERE GETTING ALONG SO WELL UNTIL I STARTED HOUSE-HUNTING AND THEN YOU JUST SORT OF DROPPED OUT.
WELL, YOU KNOW... ..I'VE BEEN BUSY..

IT SEEMS AS IF EVERY TIME THINGS REALLY START WORKING BETWEEN US, YOU TAKE OFF.
UM, WELL... I HAVE TO GO, CATHY.

LOVE IS LIKE A LEOTARD. IT EXPANDS AS FAR AS IT CAN AND THEN IT RUNS.
Guisewite

HOW WAS LUNCH, CATHY?
I PICKED A FIGHT WITH IRVING, BLEW IT INTO A HUGE ARGUMENT AND NOW WE'RE NOT SPEAKING.
CHARLENE

FRUSTRATED BY IRVING, I STOMPED INTO THE DEPARTMENT STORE, LASHED OUT WITH MY CHARGE CARD AND SPENT $200 I COULDN'T AFFORD.
CHARLENE

DISGUSTED THAT I'D RUINED MY BUDGET OVER RUINING MY RELATIONSHIP, I RACED INTO THE CROISSANT SHOP AND RUINED MY DIET.

I CAN ACCOMPLISH MORE IN ONE LUNCH HOUR THAN MOST PEOPLE CAN DO IN A MONTH.
Mall
Guisewite

THAT'S A GREAT DRESS.
THANKS, CATHY. I GOT IT TO WEAR IN CASE ANYONE ASKED ME FOR A ROMANTIC PICNIC THIS SUMMER.

I GOT THIS IN CASE I WENT OUT FOR A MOONLIT DINNER AT AN OUTDOOR CAFÉ.
I HAVE SIX DIFFERENT OUTFITS THAT WOULD BE PERFECT FOR SUMMER PARTIES I HAVEN'T BEEN INVITED TO YET.
POPCORN

WE HAVE TO MEET SOME NEW MEN, CHARLENE.
NOW! NOW WHILE SILVER SANDALS ARE STILL IN STYLE!! NOW WHILE THERE'S STILL TIME TO GET SOME ACTION FROM THE OFF-THE-SHOULDER LOOK!!
POP CORN

OUR BIOLOGICAL CLOSETS ARE TAKING OVER WHERE OUR BIOLOGICAL CLOCKS LEFT OFF.
Guisewite

I'M SO TIRED OF THEM ATTACKING OUR GENERATION FOR OUR "SELF-INDULGENT YUPPIE" MENTALITY, CATHY.
ME TOO, IRVING.

IT WAS OUR GENERATION THAT CALLED ATTENTION TO THE POVERTY OF UNDERPRIVILEGED NATIONS!
OUR GENERATION REJECTED THE CRASS CAPITALISM OF OUR PARENTS! WE MADE THE MEDIA STARS WHO FIGHT FOR THE HOMELESS!

OUR GENERATION IS RESPONSIBLE FOR RAISING THE SOCIAL CONSCIOUSNESS ENOUGH SO THAT WE COULD BE LABELED AS HYPOCRITES!!

WE'VE ALREADY DONE SO MUCH.
PASS THE REMOTE CONTROL.

AREN'T YOU WORRIED ABOUT RUNNING OUT OF TIME TO HAVE A BABY, CATHY?
SOMETIMES, SURE...I THINK IT WOULD BE SO WONDERFUL TO HAVE A BABY TO TAKE CARE OF.

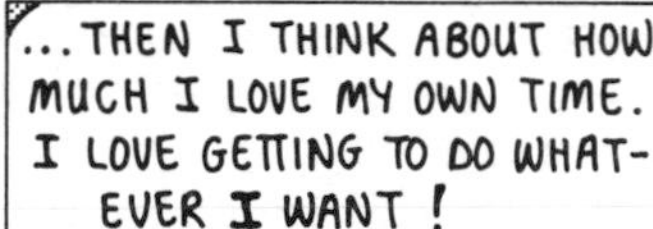
...THEN I THINK ABOUT HOW MUCH I LOVE MY OWN TIME. I LOVE GETTING TO DO WHATEVER I WANT!

MY HOUSE IS FOR ME! MY MONEY'S ALL FOR ME! MY WHOLE LIFE REVOLVES AROUND ME, AND I LOVE THAT!! ME, ME, ME!!!

I GUESS THAT'S THE POINT A LOT OF US GET TO...
YEAH...I'M TORN BETWEEN WANTING TO HAVE ONE AND WANTING TO BE ONE.

DATING IS TORTURE TODAY.
HOW DO YOU ASK WHAT YOU'RE SUPPOSED TO ASK? WHEN DO YOU ASK? WHO DO YOU BELIEVE? WHERE DO YOU GET PROOF?

WHO'S SUPPOSED TO BUY WHAT TO PREPARE FOR WHATEVER, AND HOW ON EARTH DOES ONE BUY IT??
AND HOW DOES ONE MENTION ONE HAS IT WHILE CLAIMING TO NEVER BE IN A SITUATION WHERE IT IS REQUIRED??

DATING IS REALLY TORTURE TODAY.

WE DON'T ACTUALLY KNOW ANYONE TO GO OUT WITH, CATHY.
THAT TOO.

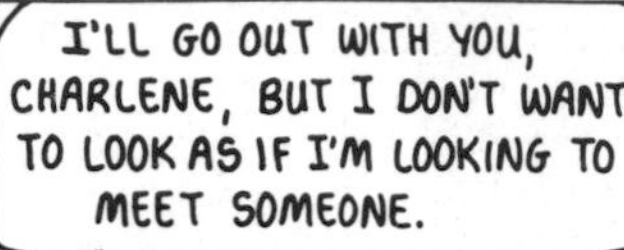

I'LL GO OUT WITH YOU, CHARLENE, BUT I DON'T WANT TO LOOK AS IF I'M LOOKING TO MEET SOMEONE.

I DON'T WANT TO LOOK, ACT, SOUND, OR SEEM AS IF I'M LOOKING.

IF I MET SOMEONE, I WOULD DENY THAT I EVER **HAD** BEEN LOOKING. I AM NOT **NOW**, **HAVE BEEN**, OR **EVER WILL BE** LOOKING. DO YOU UNDERSTAND ??
I AM NOT LOOKING !!!!

SQUIRT.
FRAUD: THE FOUNDATION OF LOVE.

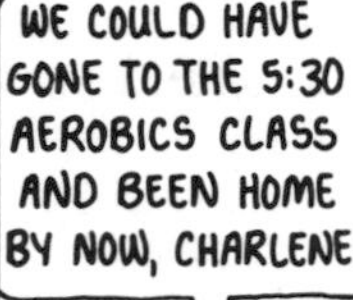

WE COULD HAVE GONE TO THE 5:30 AEROBICS CLASS AND BEEN HOME BY NOW, CHARLENE.
THERE ARE NO GOOD MEN IN THE 5:30 CLASS, CATHY.
CLASS SCHEDUL
HIGH IMPACT
LOW IMPACT

WE WANT TO MEET SOMEONE WHO'S IMPORTANT ENOUGH TO STAY AT THE OFFICE UNTIL 7:00, BUT NOT SO FANATICAL THAT HE WORKS ANY LATER. THE 7:30 CLASS IS THE POWER CLASS !

TRUST ME. OPEN THAT DOOR AND WHAT DO YOU SEE ??!!
AEROBICS

45 WOMEN IN FULL MAKEUP CHASING ONE GUY IN SHORTS.
SOMEONE BLABBED MY SYSTEM.

I FEEL LIKE AN IDIOT STANDING IN FRONT OF THE SINGLE SERVING FROZEN FOODS, CHARLENE.
TRUST ME, CATHY. THIS IS WHERE THE BACHELORS SHOP.

WE'VE BEEN STANDING HERE FOR 20 MINUTES. WHAT DO PEOPLE THINK WE'RE DOING ??
WHO ? WHO DO YOU THINK IS TIMING US ? WHO CARES WHAT WE'RE DOING ??
Lasagna

THERE'S A REAL LOOKER OVER IN THE SOUP-FOR-ONE AISLE.

DIBS !!

ALSO, YOU HAVE LASAGNA MELTING DOWN YOUR SLEEVE.
GO AWAY. I'M READING THE LABEL.

YOU DON'T KNOW WHAT IT'S LIKE FOR WOMEN IN THIS TOWN, GRANT. THERE ARE NO SINGLE MEN.
EVERY SINGLE MAN I KNOW SAYS THERE ARE NO SINGLE WOMEN.
CLEAN UP YOUR MESS

THAT FIGURES. THE ONLY MEN HERE ARE ARRO-GANT, PARANOID FLAKES!!
THE ONLY WOMEN ARE CLINGY, MATERIAL-ISTIC AIR-HEADS!!

HAH!
HAH!
OH, COME ON, YOU TWO. THERE ARE LOTS OF SINGLE MEN AND WOMEN IN TOWN.

WE JUST CAN'T STAND EACH OTHER.
Guisewite

SIMPLY WALK UP TO A CUTE GUY...ASK IF HE KNOWS HOW TO COOK EGGPLANT... AND BEFORE YOU KNOW IT, YOU'LL BE SIPPING CAPPUCCINO TOGETHER, CATHY.
IF IT'S SO EASY, YOU DO IT, CHARLENE.

HI. HEE, HEE, HEE... DO YOU KNOW HOW TO COOK EGG-PLANT ??
NO. BUT MAYBE MY WIFE OF NINE YEARS DOES.

JUDY!
HIKE!
AACK!

WHAT??
HI. HEE, HEE, HEE......
DIAPERS

IF YOU SEEM INVOLVED WITH SOMEONE AT THIS PARTY AND I WANT TO LEAVE, I'LL GIVE YOU THIS SIGNAL INDICATING THAT I'M GOING HOME WITHOUT YOU.
CHECK.

IF I SEEM INVOLVED WITH SOMEONE AND YOU WANT TO LEAVE, YOU GIVE ME THE SIGNAL INDICATING THAT YOU'RE GOING HOME WITHOUT ME.
CHECK.
103

WELL, HELLO, BEAUTIFUL!

104

SO MANY WOMEN MY AGE ARE FRANTIC TO MEET SOMEONE. I DON'T BLAME MEN FOR HAVING THEIR DEFENSES UP.
REALLY? YOU UNDER-STAND THAT??

I SEE IT ALL THE TIME. WOMEN TOTALLY MANIPU-LATE MEN INTO SITUATIONS.
YEAH... WHEW. WE HATE THAT!

I'D RATHER BE ALONE MY WHOLE LIFE THAN FEEL I'D TRICKED SOMEONE INTO A RE-LATIONSHIP WITH ME!
THAT'S SO GREAT TO HEAR!

STEP ONE: RELAX YOUR VICTIM.

SO...
NO.

NO WAY. NO. NO ATTRACTION. NO CHEMISTRY. NOTHING. NADA. ZILCH. ZERO. ZIP. NO WAY. NOT MY TYPE. NOT A CHANCE. NOTHING. NEVER. HUH, UH. NO. GONE. OVER. NEVER. EVER. NO.

MAY I HAVE YOUR PHONE NUMBER?
OK

HOW'S IT GOING, CATHY?
DON'T COME NEAR ME WITH FOOD. MY MOUTH AND MY BRAIN ARE FUNCTIONING TOTALLY INDEPENDENTLY OF EACH OTHER.
Guisewite

HAVE SOME, CATHY. YOU DON'T LOOK AS IF YOU NEED TO DIET.
ME?? WELL, I DID LOSE SOME WEIGHT THIS YEAR, BUT YOU SHOULD HAVE SEEN ME BEFORE!
REALLY? YOU??
OH, YES. I WAS FAT. ROLLS OF FAT! HA, HA. FAT AND FLAB!

...WAIT. HERE. I HAVE SOME OLD PICTURES... DO YOU BELIEVE IT?? HA, HA! LOOK AT MY FACE!! LOOK AT MY FAT ARMS! HA, HA......

...I'VE FINALLY MET A MAN WHO'S NEVER SEEN ME FAT, AND I'M GIVING HIM A SLIDE SHOW.
Guisewite

GREAT PARTY, HUH?
I GAVE MY PHONE NUMBER TO THREE MEN I WAS REPULSED BY, AND ONE I THOUGHT WAS ADORABLE.

DO I CHANGE MY PHONE NUMBER TO PROTECT MYSELF FROM THE THREE MEN I NEVER WANT TO SPEAK TO WHO WILL CALL...

...OR DO I KEEP IT THE SAME FOR THE ONE MAN I'D LOVE TO TALK TO WHO WILL NEVER CALL?
OH, HA, HA, CATHY! WHAT AN IMAGINATION!

YOU ALREADY HAVE THREE MESSAGES.
HELLO, OPERATOR? MY TELEPHONE LINE IS ABOUT TO BE SLASHED.
Guisewite

WE COULD GO OUT THERE AGAIN AND SEARCH FOR SUMMER ROMANCE IN A TOWN OF 6 MILLION SINGLE WOMEN AND 4 MEN...OR WE COULD SIT HERE EATING DOVE BARS AND DORITOS UNTIL WE PASS OUT.

WE COULD FLING OURSELVES INTO THE MOST PARANOID, UPTIGHT DATING SCENE IN THE HISTORY OF THIS COUNTRY... OR WE COULD SIT HERE COMPLIMENTING EACH OTHER AND MAKING MARSHMALLOW SANDWICHES OUT OF MRS. FIELDS COOKIES.

IT'S TOUGH OUT THERE, CATHY.
DOVE
Chocolate Chocolate Chip

IT'S EVEN WORSE IN HERE.
Guisewite

DOESN'T IT BOTHER YOU THAT ALTHOUGH WE'RE SUCCESSFUL BUSINESSWOMEN, WE HAVE THE DATING SKILLS OF A 16-YEAR-OLD?
WOMEN

THAT'S NOT TRUE, CATHY. WHEN WE WERE 16, WE'D DROP EVERYTHING AND RACE OFF AFTER THE FIRST CUTE GUY WE SAW. WE WOULDN'T DO THAT NOW!
SOAP

DO YOU KNOW **WHY** WE WOULDN'T DROP EVERYTHING AND RACE OFF AFTER THE FIRST CUTE GUY WE SAW??

BECAUSE IT TAKES US 20 MINUTES TO COVER UP ALL THE WRINKLES.
VOILÁ! MATURITY!
Guisewite

I'M SURE YOUR WORK KEEPS YOU PRETTY BUSY, BUT MAYBE I CAN CALL SOMETIME, CHARLENE.
YES! CALL! I WON'T BE BUSY!

WANT A LONG LUNCH? NO PROBLEM! WANT ME TO LEAVE WORK EARLY? NO PROBLEM! WANT ME TO PLAY HOOKEY FOR A FEW DAYS? NO PROBLEM!

WANT TO RUN OFF TO PARIS? NO PROBLEM! I'LL QUIT MY JOB! I'M GONE! I'M OUT OF THERE! **BAG THE CAREER AND TAKE ME AWAY WITH YOU!!**

NICE GOING, CHARLENE.
I WANTED HIM TO KNOW HOW MUCH MY JOB MEANS TO ME.
Guisewite

THE MOST FRUSTRATING THING ABOUT NOT MEETING A MAN IS THAT I FEEL I'M PERFECT RIGHT NOW.
ME, TOO. I'M AS THIN AND CONFIDENT AS I'VE EVER BEEN.
PASTA

I HAVE BEAUTY, BRAINS, CHARM, YOUTH, SPIRIT, HUMOR, AND I'M IN THE PERFECT WEEK OF MY PERM!
RIGHT NOW, THIS INSTANT, I AM AS GOOD AS I'M GOING TO GET!!

HI.
...WAIT...WAIT...JUST A SEC...WAIT...HOLD ON...WAIT ONE MINUTE ...ONE SEC...WAIT...
PUFF SQUIRT
PAT
POOF COMB
BRUSH PUFF

YOU'RE TOO LATE.

SO, CATHY, HAVE YOU DATED ANYONE IN, SAY, THE LAST TEN YEARS?
WELL, YES... I'VE BEEN SEEING ONE PERSON FOR A WHILE.

BUT YOU ALSO SEE OTHER PEOPLE??
WELL, YES... SOMETIMES.
YOU'RE SEEING ME RIGHT NOW.
YES. I'M SEEING YOU.

AND WHILE YOU'RE SEEING ME, IS YOUR BOYFRIEND SEEING PEOPLE AND ARE THEY PEOPLE WHO HAVE SEEN OTHER PEOPLE AND DO YOU KNOW WHAT KIND OF PEOPLE THOSE PEOPLE MIGHT HAVE SEEN???

I MISS THE GOOD OLD DAYS WHEN I COULD BE REJECTED ON MY OWN MERITS.

MY OLD COMPANY WANTS TO GIVE ME MY JOB BACK!
YOU'D GO BACK TO A PLACE THAT FIRED YOU FOR TAKING TOO MANY "VACATION DAYS" TO HAVE A BABY??

THEY'RE OBVIOUSLY RESPONDING TO THE SUPREME COURT RULING LAST WINTER THAT UPHELD A CALIFORNIA LAW SAYING EMPLOYERS HAVE TO GIVE WOMEN THEIR JOBS BACK AFTER A MATERNITY LEAVE.

IF COMPANIES ARE WAKING UP TO THE FACT THAT THEY HAVE TO TAKE PART IN THE FUTURE OF OUR FAMILIES, THEN YES! I WANT TO BE THERE! AND I WANT MY DAUGHTER TO HEAR WITH HER OWN EARS WHY A MOTHER LIKE ME CAN RECLAIM HER OWN JOB!!

THE WOMAN WHO REPLACED YOU IS HAVING A C-SECTION. SHE'LL BE CANNED WITHIN THE MONTH!
PERSONNEL

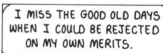

THIS COMPANY STILL HAS NO POLICY GUARANTEEING A WOMAN CAN GET HER JOB BACK IF SHE TAKES TIME OFF TO HAVE A BABY ??
WHY SHOULD WE ?
PERSONNEL

OUR NON-EXISTENT PARENTAL LEAVE POLICY WORKS IN PERFECT HARMONY WITH OUR NON-EXISTENT CHILD CARE POLICY....SINCE IF A WOMAN **COULD** GET HER JOB BACK, THERE'S NO WAY SHE COULD AFFORD DECENT CHILD CARE.

WITH OUR HELP, A WOMAN HAS HER BABY, LOSES HER JOB AND BOOM--**VOILÀ**!-- INSTANT BABY SITTER !!

INCREDIBLE.
ISN'T IT ? IT ISN'T OFTEN OUR SYSTEMS MESH SO WELL !

IF BUSINESS IS SLOW TO SUPPORT PARENTAL LEAVE POLICIES, IT'S BECAUSE WE HOLD THE **OLD-FASHIONED FAMILY UNIT** SO SACRED !
ONLY 10% OF THE FAMILIES IN THE COUNTRY LIVE IN AN OLD-FASHIONED FAMILY UNIT.

WE HOLD **MOTHERHOOD** SACRED !
67% OF MOTHERS WITH CHILDREN UNDER AGE THREE WORK FULL TIME.
PERSONNEL

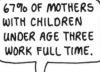

WE HOLD THE **MALE BREADWINNER** SACRED !
40% OF THE WOMEN WHO WORK ARE MARRIED TO MEN WHO EARN LESS THAN $15,000 A YEAR....

...AND ONE-FIFTH OF ALL FAMILIES HAVE NO MALE BREADWINNER AT ALL.
WE HOLD THE DAYS OF NO STATISTICAL ANALYSIS SACRED.

THE U.S. IS THE ONLY INDUSTRIALIZED NATION IN THE WORLD WITH NO FEDERAL POLICY FOR PARENTAL LEAVE.
THAT'S CORRECT ! WE **REFUSE** TO TURN INTO A "BIG BROTHER IS WATCHING YOU" KIND OF SOCIETY !

WE HAVE NO FEDERAL REGULATIONS FOR CHILD CARE.
CORRECT ! WE **ABHOR** THAT "BIG BROTHER IS WATCHING YOU" MENTALITY !
PRESIDENT

WHAT'S SUPPOSED TO HAPPEN TO THE 34 MILLION AMERICAN CHILDREN WHO HAVE MOTHERS THAT WORK ??

THEIR BIG BROTHERS ARE WATCHING THEM !!
PRESIDENT

WHEN TWO PEOPLE HAVEN'T SEEN EACH OTHER IN A WHILE, IT'S NORMAL TO FEEL STRANGE AT FIRST, IRVING.
I DON'T FEEL STRANGE. DO YOU FEEL STRANGE?

NO, I DON'T FEEL STRANGE, BUT I WOULDN'T WANT YOU JUDGING OUR WHOLE RELATIONSHIP ON THIS ONE EVENING IF YOU FELT STRANGE.
I DON'T FEEL STRANGE, CATHY.

I JUST THOUGHT YOU MIGHT FEEL THAT I FEEL STRANGE, WHICH I DON'T, BUT IF I DID, IT WOULDN'T BE STRANGE ABOUT YOU, JUST THAT IT'S A NORMAL STRANGE SITUATION.
FINE.

PLEASE, GOD, LET THERE BE SOMETHING GOOD ON TELEVISION.
Guisewite

NEW MOTHERS ARE THE ONES MOST AWARE OF THE NEED FOR THE PARENTAL AND MEDICAL LEAVE ACT, BUT WE'RE TOO EXHAUSTED AND FRAZZLED TO WRITE LETTERS OF SUPPORT.

FEED THE BABIES... CHANGE THE BABIES... CHASE THE BABIES... RACE TO THE GROCERY STORE... RACE TO THE BABY SITTER... RACE TO THE JOB... RACE TO THE DOCTOR... WASH THE CLOTHES... IT'S ENDLESS....

IF YOU COULD JUST WATCH ZENITH FOR FIVE MINUTES, I COULD GO IN THERE AND FINALLY START A SHOW OF SUPPORT OUR CONGRESSPEOPLE AND SENATORS HAVE NEVER SEEN BEFORE!!!

THE 1987 FACE-PRINT CAMPAIGN.
Z Z Z Z Z Z Z Z Z Z Z Z

I INVITED THE MOTHERS AND CHILDREN OF ZENITH'S PLAY GROUP OVER TO HELP WRITE LETTERS SUPPORTING THE PARENTAL LEAVE ACT, CATHY.
THAT'S GREAT.

IT'S MORE THAN GREAT. THIS IS AMERICA IN ACTION... THE KIND OF SCENE THAT MADE OUR COUNTRY WHAT IT IS TODAY...

MOTHERS WRITING LETTERS FOR A CAUSE THEY BELIEVE IN!

...AND THEIR CHILDREN EATING THEM.

THREE CALLS FROM CLIENTS, TWO FROM YOUR MOM, AND ONE FROM LEONARD.
NOT LEONARD FROM THE PARTY.
RECEPTIONIST

LEONARD FROM THE PARTY.
I CHANGED MY HOME PHONE NUMBER SO LEONARD FROM THE PARTY COULDN'T CALL!
RECEPTIONIST

CATHY, I'M SURE WE'VE EVOLVED TO A POINT WHERE WE CAN FIND WAYS TO DEAL WITH PEOPLE BESIDES CHANGING OUR HOME PHONE NUMBERS!
RIGHT...
RECEPTIONIST

MR. PINKLEY, WE HAVE TO CHANGE THE NAME, ADDRESS AND PHONE NUMBER OF OUR COMPANY.

YOU AGREED TO DINNER AND A MOVIE WITH A MAN YOU DON'T LIKE, CATHY?
I HAD TO. I TURNED HIM DOWN FOR DRINKS FOUR TIMES.
MILK

WHAT DOES THAT HAVE TO DO WITH IT??
IT'S THE MULTIPLICATION TABLE OF GUILT, MOM.

TURN A MAN DOWN FOR DRINKS TWICE AND YOU OWE HIM LUNCH... TURN HIM DOWN FOR LUNCH, YOU OWE HIM DINNER... TURN HIM DOWN FOR LUNCH AND DRINKS, YOU OWE HIM SUNDAY BRUNCH.

THAT'S RIDICULOUS. JUST CALL AND SAY YOU CAN'T MAKE IT.
IF I CANCEL DINNER AND A MOVIE, I HAVE TO MARRY HIM.
MILK
Guisewite

I COULDN'T BELIEVE YOU AGREED TO GO OUT WITH ME, CATHY!
...YOU COULDN'T BELIEVE I AGREED TO GO OUT WITH YOU, LEONARD??

I DIDN'T REALLY THINK I WAS YOUR TYPE.
AHEM... YOU DIDN'T THINK YOU WERE MY TYPE??

BUT YOU MUST HAVE FELT SOMETHING, BECAUSE HERE WE ARE!!
YES... AHEM... PARDON ME FOR A MOMENT... I HAVE SOMETHING STUCK IN MY THROAT.....

...I COULD HAVE SAID NO!!!
TOWELS
SOAP
Guisewite

WANT TO STOP OVER AND SEE MY PLACE, CATHY?
NO. I DON'T WANT TO SEE HIS PLACE. I NEVER WANT TO SEE HIM AFTER TONIGHT.

NO. I'VE FULFILLED MY OBLIGATION. I SAID MAYBE I'D GO OUT, AND I'VE GONE OUT. I TRIED. NOW I'M FINISHED. NO MORE. I OWE HIM NOTHING. AFTER TONIGHT, IT'S OVER! AFTER TONIGHT, I'M FREE!!

HO, HUM... I THINK I'D RATHER JUST GO HOME, LEONARD.
OK, BUT YOU HAVE TO PROMISE TO STOP OVER NEXT TIME!

NO! TAKE ME THERE NOW!! LET'S GET IT OVER WITH NOW!!
I LOVE IT WHEN THEY GET A SECOND WIND.
Guisewite

WILL YOU HAVE DINNER WITH ME SUNDAY?
NO. NO, I JUST CAN'T. THIS IS SO HARD TO SAY, BUT I WANT TO BE HONEST WITH YOU, LEONARD.

I JUST DON'T FEEL THAT SPECIAL SPARK BETWEEN US. IT WOULD BE WRONG TO HAVE DINNER AGAIN. I HAVE NO INTEREST IN GETTING INVOLVED.

COULDN'T WE JUST BE FRIENDS?
WELL, YES...OF COURSE WE CAN BE FRIENDS.
COULDN'T YOU HAVE DINNER WITH ME SUNDAY AS MY FRIEND?
WELL, YES. OF COURSE. DINNER AS A FRIEND.

GREAT. THEN IT'S A DATE!
WHAT HAPPENED?

SOMETIMES WOMEN LIE AND SAY THEY HAVE ANOTHER BOYFRIEND WHEN THEY DON'T WANT TO GO OUT WITH ME, CATHY.
REALLY? THAT'S TERRIBLE.

SOME WOMEN LIE AND SAY THEY'RE LEAVING THE COUNTRY FOR TWO MONTHS.... SOME LIE AND SAY THEY WORK UNTIL MIDNIGHT....SOME LIE AND SAY THEY'RE SICK...OR THEIR MOTHER'S SICK...OR THEIR WHOLE FAMILY'S SICK...

I JUST KNOW YOU'D NEVER DO THAT.
ME? NO. NO CHANCE OF THAT.

HOW'S LEONARD?
HE'S TOO EXPERIENCED FOR ME.

SUDDENLY, I'M "DATING" A MAN I NEVER EVEN WANTED TO TALK TO... MY MOM'S SENDING ANONYMOUS "DEAR ABBY" CLIPPINGS TO MY REAL BOYFRIEND, WHO SHE SAW HAVING LUNCH WITH AN OLD GIRLFRIEND..

MY BOSS SNEAKED IN WHILE I WAS DISTRACTED ABOUT MY LOVE LIFE AND GOT ME TO PROMISE TO DO A TWO-WEEK PROJECT IN ONE NIGHT.... PEOPLE ARE RUNNING MY LIFE, ANDREA!

CATHY, I THINK THE PROBLEM IS A LITTLE DEEPER THAN "PEOPLE RUNNING YOUR LIFE."
YEAH...I GUESS YOU'RE RIGHT...

PEOPLE AREN'T RUNNING MY LIFE THE WAY I **WANT** THEM TO RUN MY LIFE!!!

HOW ARE YOU GOING TO BREAK IT TO LEONARD THAT THIS IS YOUR LAST DATE, CATHY?
LEONARD AND I HAVE NOTHING IN COMMON. IT'S AS SIMPLE AS THAT.

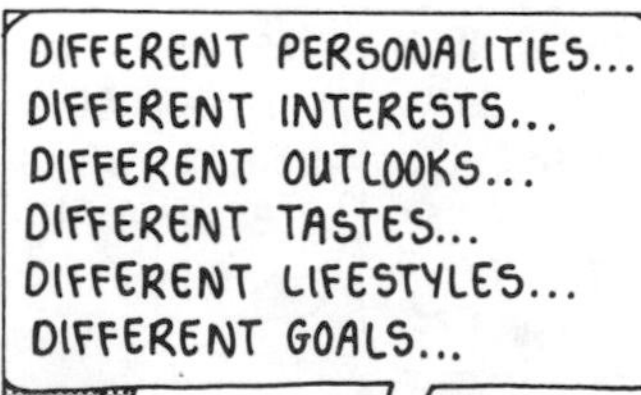
DIFFERENT PERSONALITIES... DIFFERENT INTERESTS... DIFFERENT OUTLOOKS... DIFFERENT TASTES... DIFFERENT LIFESTYLES... DIFFERENT GOALS...

LOOK, CATHY!! WE HAVE THE SAME NUMBER OF LETTERS IF YOU ADD UP OUR FIRST AND LAST NAMES...WE BOTH HAVE THE MOON IN LIBRA... AND THE TOWNS WE'RE FROM HAVE TWO OF THE SAME DIGITS IN THE ZIP CODES!!

THAT'S EXACTLY THE SORT OF THING YOU'D DO, CATHY.
HELP ME, CHARLENE.

I'VE ALWAYS BEEN SO INSECURE WITH WOMEN, BUT I FEEL CONFIDENT WITH YOU, CATHY.
OH, NO. DON'T KISS ME, LEONARD.

I'M USUALLY SO AWKWARD, BUT WITH YOU I CAN JUST BE MYSELF...
DON'T EVEN THINK ABOUT KISSING ME! NO KISSING! THINGS ARE BAD ENOUGH. DON'T EVEN CONSIDER...

KISS

AAACK!!
WHEW! IF ONE KISS GETS YOU THAT EXCITED, IMAGINE WHAT LIES AHEAD!!

JUST TELL LEONARD THERE'S SOMEONE ELSE, CATHY!
I HATE HOW SMUG YOU ARE ABOUT THIS, CHARLENE. IT ISN'T THAT EASY.

JUST MAKE SOMEONE UP! INVENT SOMEONE! JUST SAY THERE'S SOMEONE ELSE!

LEONARD, CHARLENE'S BEEN TALKING ABOUT YOU EVER SINCE SHE SAW YOU AT THAT PARTY... AND I FEEL I CAN NO LONGER STAND BETWEEN THE FUTURE YOU TWO MAY HAVE TOGETHER.

CHARLENE?? REALLY?! CHARLENE'S INTERESTED?!

DID YOU TELL HIM THERE'S SOMEONE ELSE?
YES, AND HE WANTS TO SPEAK TO YOU.

I'M MOVING IN A WEEK AND WANT TO CHECK ON A COUCH I ORDERED.
CERTAINLY. WHEN DID YOU PLACE YOUR ORDER?
CATHY

JUNE 1985.
AH, YES. THAT SHOULD BE IN ANY DAY NOW.
CATHY

YOU'VE BEEN SAYING IT SHOULD BE IN ANY DAY FOR TWO YEARS!!
YES. WELL, NOW IT SHOULD REALLY, REALLY BE IN ANY DAY.
CATHY

YOU'RE GETTING A NEW COUCH, CATHY??
I ORDERED A NEW COUCH. I'LL BE GETTING AN ANTIQUE.
CATHY

TAKE YOUR HAND FROM YOUR FACE, MA'AM. IT ISN'T THAT BAD.
WHEN I CAME IN TO CHECK ON THE COUCH I ORDERED TWO YEARS AGO, YOU TALKED ME INTO A TABLE THAT WON'T BE IN FOR NINE MONTHS.
FURNITURE

WHEN I CAME IN TO CHECK ON THE TABLE, YOU MADE ME FALL IN LOVE WITH A DINING ROOM SET I WON'T SEE FOR ANOTHER TEN MONTHS.

I AM NOT LOOKING AT ANOTHER PIECE OF FURNITURE UNTIL WHAT I'VE ALREADY ORDERED HAS ARRIVED!!
OF COURSE. HERE. SIT DOWN AND I'LL FIND YOUR PAPERWORK.

OOH... THIS IS NICE! HOW LONG?
SIX TO EIGHT WEEKS.

I WANT TO KNOW WHAT HAPPENED TO THE COUCH I ORDERED TWO YEARS AGO.
THE COMPUTER WENT BERSERK AND THE SHIPMENT GOT BACKED UP.
6-8 WEEK DELIVERY (USUALLY)
FURNITURE ORDERS

I'VE ALREADY HEARD THAT ONE.
THE BOAT SANK.
I'VE HEARD THAT ONE.
THE FABRIC CUTTERS WENT ON STRIKE.
I'VE HEARD THAT ONE.

THE FOREMAN GOT IN A FIGHT WITH HIS BOSS AND RIPPED UP THE ORDERS WHILE, SIMULTANEOUSLY, THE FRAME SUPPLIER WENT BELLY-UP AND AUCTIONED OFF THEIR ENTIRE INVENTORY!!

HEARD IT.
EVERY YEAR I SPEND IN THE FURNITURE BUSINESS, IT GETS HARDER TO COME UP WITH A WHOLE NEW LINE.
6-8 WEEK DELIVERY (USUALLY)
FURNITURE ORDERS

I'VE BEEN CALLING, CATHY... YOU'RE NEVER THERE.
I'VE BEEN OUT, IRVING. OUT MEETING MEN.

MEN?
NEW MEN. LOTS OF MEN! FASCINATING MEN! CHARMING MEN!! MEN I WILL BE SPENDING A GREAT DEAL OF TIME WITH!!!

ARE YOU FREE TONIGHT?
YES.

THAT'S THE PROBLEM WITH MEN. THEY UNDERSTAND EACH OTHER.
Guisewite

WHAT SHOULD I DO, MOM? I'M SUPPOSED TO MOVE IN A WEEK, AND THE FURNITURE I ORDERED TWO YEARS AGO STILL HASN'T SHOWN UP.

I'LL MARCH DOWN TO THAT STORE AND DEMAND SERVICE! I'LL WRITE THE BETTER BUSINESS BUREAU! I'LL ORGANIZE MY FRIENDS AND PICKET THE SHOPPING CENTER!!

I'LL SPEAK TO THE MANAGER, THE SUPERVISOR AND THE PRESIDENT OF THE COMPANY, AND THEN I'LL PLANT MYSELF IN A DISPLAY MODEL AND NOT BUDGE UNTIL I GET ACTION!!

IF YOU'D ASK FOR HELP MORE OFTEN, I COULD LET IT OUT IN SMALLER DOSES.
Boycott

I'M SORRY IT'S COME TO THIS, BUT MY MOTHER IS IRATE ABOUT YOUR INABILITY TO GET MY FURNITURE DELIVERED.
ONE MOMENT.

MOM!

MY DAUGHTER HAS BEEN WAITING FOR HER SOFA FOR TWO YEARS!
MY DAUGHTER IS SICK OF GETTING BLAMED FOR EVERY TEENSY DELAY!!

MY DAD'S OUT IN THE CAR.
MINE'S WAITING IN THE BACK ROOM.

PICTURE OF THE CONDOMINIUM I BOUGHT BUT CAN'T GO INTO BECAUSE ESCROW HASN'T CLOSED.

PICTURE OF THE CARPETING AND BLINDS I PAID FOR BUT CAN'T HAVE BECAUSE I CAN'T LET THE INSTALLERS IN THE CONDOMINIUM I CAN'T GET INTO.

PICTURES OF FURNITURE I OWN BUT CAN'T SIT ON, EAT OFF OF OR USE BECAUSE IT'S ALL LOST SOMEWHERE IN OVERDUE DELIVERY LAND.

FOR SOMEONE WHO'S JUST PLUNGED HERSELF HOPELESSLY INTO DEBT FOR THE REST OF HER LIFE, I LOOK PRETTY GOOD ON PAPER.

I'LL BET YOU HAVEN'T EVEN STARTED GETTING READY TO MOVE, HAVE YOU, CATHY ?
HAH! LOOK AT THIS, MOM. TEN BOXES PACKED!

YOUR MOVE IS A WEEK AWAY AND YOU ALREADY HAVE TEN BOXES PACKED ??
MISC.

THIS CAN MEAN ONLY ONE THING !
MISC.

THESE ARE BOXES YOU NEVER UNPACKED FROM THE LAST TIME YOU MOVED!
IT'S HARD TO IMPRESS THEM ONCE THEY GET TO KNOW YOU..
MISC.

PACKING DAY #1: METICULOUSLY WRAP EACH ITEM AND PLACE IN BOX BY WEIGHT. LIST CONTENTS ON BOX WITH PHOTOCOPY CROSS-REFERENCED TO ALPHABETIZED MASTER LIST, INCLUDING COMPLETE PLACEMENT INSTRUCTIONS FOR NEW HOME.

TISSUE PAPER

PACKING DAY #2: FLING ANYTHING I SEE INTO ANY BOX THAT'S OPEN.
MISC.

PACKING DAY #3: START BREAKING THINGS SO I DON'T HAVE TO DEAL WITH THEM.
SMASH!
CRUNCH!
COOKIES

PACKING DAY #4: HIRE A PROFESSIONAL.
Hello, Doctor? I'm ready to begin my therapy now.

BOXES OF CLOTHES...
BASKETS OF CLOTHES...
TRUNKS OF CLOTHES...
CRATES OF CLOTHES...
BAGS OF CLOTHES...
HAMPERS OF CLOTHES...
HEAPS OF CLOTHES...

I CAN'T BELIEVE THIS, MOM.
I KNOW WHAT YOU MEAN, CATHY.

HOW CAN YOU SAY YOU HAVE NOTHING TO WEAR ?

HOW DID ALL THIS COME OUT OF A HOME WITH NO CLOSET SPACE ??!

OH, DARN. I HAVE TO GO GET MORE BOXES.
YOU'RE JUST TRYING TO GET OUT OF PACKING.

I HAPPEN TO NEED MORE BOXES, MOTHER.
IT'S CLASSIC. A PERSON LEAVES THE MESS AND THEN WASTES THE DAY DOING NOTHING THAT HAS TO DO WITH MOVING, CATHY.

IF YOU'RE GOING TO GET BOXES, I WILL GO WITH YOU TO MAKE SURE YOU GET BOXES!!

...WELL, WE GOT BOXES.
THEY JUST HAPPEN TO BE FULL OF SHOES ALREADY...

SHOULDN'T YOUR BOYFRIEND BE HELPING YOU PACK, CATHY?
I DON'T WANT MY BOYFRIEND TO SEE ALL MY JUNK.

WHAT ABOUT ANDREA AND CHARLENE ?
I DON'T WANT MY GIRLFRIENDS TO SEE ALL MY JUNK.

YOU'RE THE ONLY PEOPLE IN THE WORLD THAT I WOULD LET ROOT THROUGH THE GARBAGE OF MY LIFE, MOM AND DAD!

WAS THAT A COMPLIMENT ?
WE TAKE WHAT WE CAN GET, DEAR.

I CAN'T BELIEVE I'M PACKING THIS UGLY THING AGAIN. I DON'T LIKE IT. I NEVER USE IT. I LUG IT WITH ME EVERY TIME I MOVE AND THEN HAVE TO FIND A PLACE TO STORE IT.

IT'S USELESS, MEANINGLESS AND WORTHLESS. THE ONLY TIME I EVER EVEN LOOK AT IT IS ONCE EVERY FOUR YEARS WHEN I ASK MYSELF WHY I HAVE IT.

WHY DON'T YOU JUST GIVE IT AWAY ?

I DON'T WANT TO ADMIT I WASTED MY MONEY.

BEFORE THE WRAP-UP OF A REAL ESTATE SALE, I LIKE TO REVIEW TERMS WITH MY BUYERS SO THERE'LL BE NO SURPRISES ON THE BIG DAY, CATHY.
GREAT.
NEW LISTING
LIVING SPACE SPECIALIST

FIRST TERM: "CLOSING DAY." IT'S CALLED CLOSING DAY BECAUSE IT'S NOT ONLY THE DAY YOU HAVE TO CLOSE ALL YOUR SAVINGS AND CHECKING ACCOUNTS TO COME UP WITH THE CASH... BUT IT'S ALSO THE DAY YOU CLOSE OFF ALL GOOD RELATIONS WITH FRIENDS AND FAMILY MEMBERS FROM WHOM YOU'RE BORROWING MONEY.

...AND, OF COURSE, IT'S THE DAY YOU FOREVER CLOSE THE DOOR ON THE CAREFREE LIFE OF AN APARTMENT DWELLER AND HURL YOURSELF INTO A VAT OF DEBT FROM WHICH YOU WILL NEVER ESCAPE!

AAACK!!
SECOND TERM: "BUYER'S REMORSE"...
NEW LISTING
LIVING SPACE SPECI
Guisewite

ON CLOSING DAY FOR YOUR CONDO, I'LL NEED YOUR CHECK FROM THE MORTGAGE COMPANY, CATHY.
CERTAINLY.
NEW LISTING
LIVING SPACE SPECIALIST

THEN I'LL NEED CHECKS FOR: CITY TAXES... COUNTY TAXES... ACCRUED INTEREST... HAZARD INSURANCE... MORTGAGE INSURANCE... CONDO ASSOCIATION FEE...

APPRAISAL FEE...
LOAN ORIGINATION FEE...
LOAN DISCOUNT FEE...
LOAN TIE-IN FEE...
CREDIT REPORT FEE...
TAX SERVICE FEE...
SUB-ESCROW FEE...
ANNUAL ASSESSMENT FEE...
NOTARY FEE...
ATTORNEY FEE...
DOCUMENT PREP FEE...
RECORDING FEE...
TITLE SEARCH FEE...
TITLE EXAMINATION FEE...
TITLE INSURANCE FEE...

...AND, OF COURSE, THE PARAMEDIC FEE.
CIALIST
Guisewite

I KNOW YOU'VE ALREADY HAD A LOT OF FINANCIAL SHOCKS THIS WEEK, CATHY... BUT THERE'S BEEN A TEENSY RAISE IN INTEREST RATES SINCE YOU APPLIED FOR YOUR HOME LOAN.
THERE'S BEEN A TEENSY RAISE?
REAL ESTATE CLOSING DEPARTMENT
FORMS
TISSUES

YOUR MORTGAGE PAYMENT WILL BE $300 A MONTH MORE THAN WE CALCULATED.
MY PAYMENT WILL BE $300 A MONTH **MORE**??

IT TOOK THEM TWO MONTHS TO DECIDE I COULD COME UP WITH $1,000 A MONTH, AND NOW THEY'RE MAKING ME PAY **$1,300** A MONTH ??!

BUT YOU DID IT! YOU'RE APPROVED! **THE DAY EVERY WOMAN DREAMS OF IS YOURS!**
WHEEL ME OVER THE THRESHOLD, MOTHER.
DEED
Guisewite

ALMOST NO ONE IS PREPARED FOR THE TRAUMA OF MOVING TO A NEW HOME.

IT ISN'T JUST FACING EVERY POSSESSION, BUT SEEING OUR WHOLE BASE OF SECURITY RIPPED APART AND PILED INTO A HOPELESS MESS.

SOME REACT BY SCREAMING AT ALL AROUND THEM... SOME CRY UNCONTROLLABLY.... THE BRAVEST AMONG US TAKE THAT SAME PENT-UP ENERGY OF A MILLION MEMORIES AND FLING IT INTO THE ONE BREAKTHROUGH COPING MECHANISM OF THE TWENTIETH CENTURY:

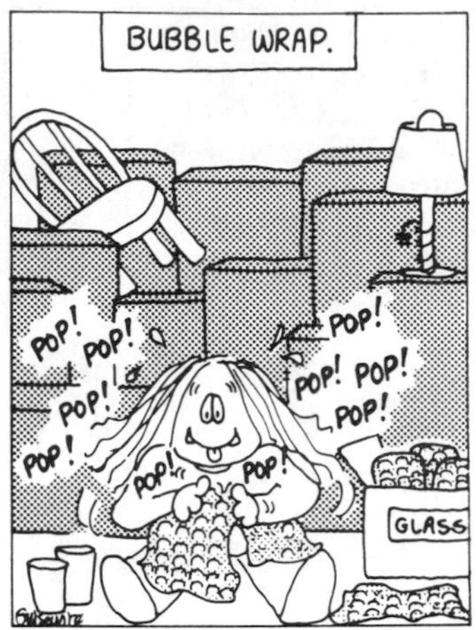

IF I CAN'T UNPACK SILVERWARE UNTIL YOU BUY ORGANIZER TRAYS, AT LEAST I CAN UNPACK DISHES.

YOU CAN'T UNPACK DISHES UNTIL I GET SHELF PAPER.

DISHES
GLASS
DISHES
GLASS
DISHES

GET SHELF PAPER LATER, CATHY.
I WON'T DO IT LATER.
THEN GET SHELF PAPER NOW.
THE PAPER I WANT IS ON ORDER.
USE A DIFFERENT KIND OF PAPER!
GLASS

IRVING, THERE ARE A MILLION THINGS TO UNPACK. WOULD YOU QUIT FIXATING ON ONES THAT REQUIRE ORGANIZER TRAYS AND SHELF PAPER??!

FINE. I'LL HANG UP CLOTHES.
YOU CAN'T HANG UP CLOTHES UNTIL I BUY MATCHING PLASTIC HANGERS.
MISC.
PANS

...NO... WAIT... THE BOXES OF BOOKS I NEVER READ GO HERE, NEXT TO THE RECORDS I NEVER LISTEN TO ON THESE SHELVES I'M GOING TO GET RID OF, BESIDE THE LAMP I HATE.

THE CRATES OF CLOTHES I HAVEN'T WORN IN FIVE YEARS GO OVER HERE WITH THE WALL HANGINGS I CAN'T STAND AND THE CARTONS OF KNICKKNACKS I HAVEN'T OPENED SINCE 1972.

EVERY TIME I MOVE, MY HOME IS MORE OF AN EXPRESSION OF WHO I REALLY AM...

I SPENT A FORTUNE ON CLOTHES TO IMPRESS HIM: ZERO IMPACT.

I READ A HUNDRED BOOKS ON HOW TO DRAW HIM CLOSER TO ME: ZILCH.

NOW HE'S STARTING TO WORRY ABOUT GOING BALD, AND SUDDENLY HE'S RUSHING TO ME FOR SECURITY AND TALKING ABOUT OUR FUTURE TOGETHER.

ALL THAT TIME I SPENT PULLING MY HAIR OUT, I SHOULD HAVE BEEN PULLING **HIS** OUT.

EVERYONE'S STARTING TO WEAR SHORT SKIRTS TO THE OFFICE, CATHY.

NOT I. A SHORT SKIRT JUST INVITES MEN TO THINK ABOUT YOUR LEGS, CHARLENE.

THE MINI-SKIRT IS A GRAND NEW SYMBOL OF THE PROGRESS WE'VE ALL MADE...MEN FINALLY RESPECT US ENOUGH AS INTELLIGENT EQUALS THAT WE CAN RELAX THE HARSHER DRESS CODES OF THE '70s AND EXPRESS OUR FEMININITY MORE FREELY!!

I'VE FINALLY PERFECTED ALL THE RIGHT IMAGES.

The '80s Woman

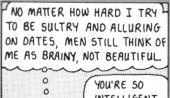

THE FANTASY: A CLOSET FULL OF STYLISH CLOTHES IN MY CURRENT SIZE, LINED UP, ALTERED, CLEANED AND READY TO DASH OFF TO ANY BUSINESS OR SOCIAL FUNCTION THAT MAY ARISE.

THE DREAM: A FEW SNAPPY OUTFITS THAT DON'T NEED IRONING.

THE PRAYER: ONE CLEAN THING THAT FITS THAT I CAN ACCESSORIZE AT THE DRUGSTORE ON THE WAY TO WORK.

THE REALITY:
FWOMP!
THE LAYERED LOOK LIVES...

I HAVE A CLOSET FULL OF CLOTHES AND NOTHING TO WEAR.
WE UNDERSTAND.
MAXI
MINI

SEE? WE HAVE A STORE FULL OF CLOTHES AND NOTHING ANYONE WANTS TO BUY!
MAXI
MINI

EVERYTHING'S TOO SHORT, TOO LONG, TOO BAGGY, TOO SQUASHY, TOO COMMON OR TOO WEIRD... ... JUST LIKE HOME! JUST THINK OF OUR STORE AS ONE GIANT, HOPELESS CLOSET!!

OH, WHAT THE HECK... I GUESS I COULD WEAR THIS...
KNOW HOW THEY LIVE, AND YOU'LL KNOW HOW THEY SHOP...
MAXI
MINI

A SIMPLE SKIRT LIKE THIS GOES WITH EVERYTHING!
YES! IT WOULD BE PERFECT WITH A BLAZER I GOT LAST YEAR!
New Fall Fashions

NOT REALLY. SHORT SKIRTS REQUIRE A LONG BLAZER.
I HAVE A LONG BLAZER.
A LONG BLAZER WITH A CINCHED WAIST AND NO LAPELS.
I'LL WEAR IT WITH MY LONG SWEATER.

NO. BLAZERS HAVE TO BE LONG. SWEATERS HAVE TO BE SHORT.
I'LL WEAR IT WITH A BLOUSE I ALREADY HAVE.
IF YOU BOUGHT THE BLOUSE BEFORE SEPTEMBER, THE COLLAR WILL BE TOO POINTY.

I THOUGHT YOU SAID THIS GOES WITH EVERYTHING.
IT GOES WITH EVERYTHING WE HAVE, NOT EVERYTHING YOU HAVE.
New Fall Fashions

I TRIED WEAR-ING THIS MINI-SKIRT TO WORK, BUT I LOOKED RIDICULOUS.
OF COURSE YOU DID. YOU CAN'T WEAR A MINISKIRT WITH NUDE PANTYHOSE.

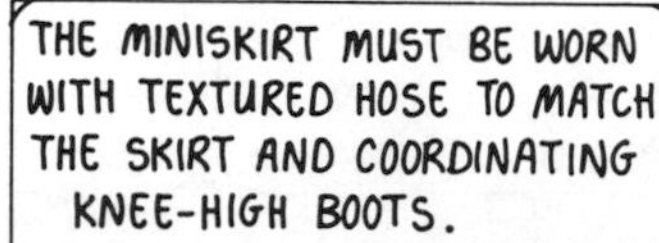
THE MINISKIRT MUST BE WORN WITH TEXTURED HOSE TO MATCH THE SKIRT AND COORDINATING KNEE-HIGH BOOTS.

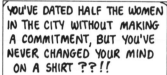

I PAID $125 FOR 12 INCHES OF FABRIC AND NOW I HAVE TO SPEND ANOTHER $400 ON LEGGINGS AND BOOTS TO COV-ER UP WHAT I BOUGHT THIS SKIRT TO SHOW OFF??!!
TA DA!

I'M STARTING TO UNDERSTAND WHY THE MINISKIRT IS A SIGN OF A STRONG ECONOMY.
Guisewite

DON'T YOU HATE IT WHEN YOU BUY CLOTHES, CHANGE YOUR MIND, AND THEN HAVE TO RETURN THEM?
I NEVER RETURN CLOTHES, CATHY.

WHAT DO YOU MEAN, YOU NEVER RETURN CLOTHES, IRVING?
IF I LIKE SOME-THING ENOUGH TO TAKE IT HOME, I KEEP IT FOR THE REST OF MY LIFE.

YOU'VE DATED HALF THE WOMEN IN THE CITY WITHOUT MAKING A COMMITMENT, BUT YOU'VE NEVER CHANGED YOUR MIND ON A SHIRT??!!

...MY BOYFRIEND: THE CLOSET MONOGAMIST.
Guisewite

I DON'T UNDER-STAND THE FASHION RULES THIS FALL.
THERE ARE NO RULES.

THIS YEAR YOU CAN WEAR SKIN-TIGHT SPANDEX LEG-GINGS WITH A BALLOONY TOP...
OR, WEAR A SKIN-TIGHT SPAN-DEX TOP WITH A BAL-LOONY SKIRT.

FOR THE FIRST TIME IN FASHION HISTORY, YOU CAN SELECT THE PART OF YOUR BODY YOU WANT TO LOOK RIDICULOUS!!

EVERY TIME THEY GIVE US MORE CHOICES, THINGS GET WORSE.
Guisewite

WHY DO WOMEN MAKE SUCH A BIG DEAL OF PULLING TOGETHER THEIR FALL WARDROBES, CATHY? LET'S JUST GO OUT RIGHT NOW AND GET IT OVER WITH.
GREAT.

I NEED A BLOUSE TO GO WITH THIS SKIRT... EARRINGS TO GO WITH THE BLOUSE... SHOES TO GO WITH THESE PANTS... A SWEATER TO MATCH THIS JACKET TO UPDATE THE SUIT TO COORDINATE WITH THE LEGGINGS... GLOVES TO GO WITH THE COAT... A COAT TO GO WITH THE BOOTS... A BRACELET TO TIE IN THE VEST WITH THE BLOUSE...

WHAT DO YOU NEED TO PULL TOGETHER **YOUR** FALL WARDROBE?
SOME BROWN SOCKS.

I'LL MEET YOU BACK HERE ON DECEMBER 3.
Guisewite

101... 102... 103. GASP! ..PUFF...
I CAN'T BELIEVE HOW DILIGENT YOU ARE, IRVING.
diet

105... 106... I'M NOT EXACTLY GETTING YOUNGER, CATHY.
I ONLY **COMPLAIN** ABOUT THE CONDITION I'M IN... YOU'RE REALLY TAKING ACTION.

...109...110... A GUY HAS TO DO WHAT A GUY HAS TO DO.
YOU'RE SUCH AN INSPIRATION TO ME!

...113... 114. GASP! 115...116......
DAILY HAIR COUNT
Guisewite

CAN YOU TELL MY HAIR IS THINNING, CATHY?
NO. DO YOU THINK MY SKIN IS SAGGING, IRVING?

NO. ARE MY WHISKERS LOOKING GRAY?
NO. AM I GETTING MORE WRINKLES?
NO. DOES MY STOMACH LOOK FAT?
NO. HAVE MY ARMS GOTTEN FLABBY?

NO! YOU LOOK **VERY** YOUNG! WE **BOTH** LOOK YOUNG! **WE'LL ALWAYS LOOK YOUNG!!**

AGING: THE LIE THAT BINDS.
Guisewite

IT TOOK ALL DAY, BUT I FOUND THE PERFECT EARRINGS TO GO WITH THIS DRESS! TA DA!
IT TOOK YOU A WHOLE DAY TO PUT TOGETHER AN OUTFIT?

ARE YOU KID-DING?? I WORKED ON FINDING THE SHOES, PURSE AND BELT FOR A MONTH!
IF A MAN CAN'T GET EVERYTHING IN FIVE MIN-UTES, HE HAS THE SENSE TO GO HOME.

I CAN'T BELIEVE YOU'D WASTE A WHOLE MONTH PUTTING TO-GETHER ONE THING! THIS IS WHY WOMEN WILL NEVER GET ANYWHERE, CATHY!!

THIS IS WHY MEN WILL NEVER GIVE BIRTH.
Guisewite

MR. PINKLEY, I ALREADY HAVE TWENTY HOURS OF WORK TO DO TODAY... I CAN'T POSSIBLY DO ALL THIS, TOO.

OF COURSE YOU CAN, CATHY. IT'S A SIMPLE MATTER OF TIME MANAGEMENT.

GO SLOWER! GO SLOWER!
TICK TICK
TICK TICK
TICK TICK
9:30
IN
IN
IN
Guisewite

EMERGENCY! I NEED THIS BY NOON!
I NEED THIS BY 1:00!
I NEED THIS BY 12:30!

SOMEONE FIND THE BRODER FILE!
SOMEONE RETYPE THE HACKETT REVISION!
SOMEONE PRINT THE SPREADSHEET AND PREP THE FAX!!

NEVER MIND! I'LL FIND IT MYSELF!!
I'LL TYPE IT MYSELF!!
I'LL PRINT AND PREP IT MYSELF!!

WE'RE NEVER ALONE IN BUSINESS. WE'RE JUST BY OURSELVES IN BIGGER GROUPS.
Guisewite

HELLO?!
OOPS. IT SOUNDS AS IF THIS IS A BAD TIME TO TALK, SWEETIE.
RING RING RING!
IN

OH, SORRY.. NO. IT'S FINE, MOM.
NO. I CAN TELL THIS ISN'T A GOOD TIME TO TALK.
PLEASE TALK. I WANT TO TALK.
YOU'RE TOO BUSY TO TALK.
IT'S OK. LET'S TALK.
WE'LL TALK LATER.

I CAN TALK NOW. I WANT TO TALK. PLEASE TALK! PLEASE! PLEASE TALK TO ME!!
IN

DO I DO THIS TO ANNOY HER, OR DO I JUST LIKE TO HEAR HER BEG FOR HER MOTHER?
Guisewite

NO, I DID NOT HAVE TIME TO WORK OUT AFTER THE OFFICE! MY DAY WAS WILD, IRVING!!
RELAX, CATHY. IT'S OVER. LET'S JUST HAVE A NICE DINNER.

IT WAS PANDEMONIUM... PHONES RINGING... PEOPLE SHRIEKING... EMERGENCIES EVERY SECOND!!
IT'S DONE. JUST RELAX.

YOU DON'T UNDERSTAND HOW CRAZY IT WAS! MISERY! HYSTERIA!! MASS CHAOS!!!
AACK! MISERY! MASS CHAOS! AACK!!

WHEW! THANKS. NOW LET'S HAVE A NICE DINNER.
IRVING: THE HUMAN HEALTH CLUB.

BELGIAN CHOCOLATE TRUFFLES MOLDED INTO JACK-O'-LANTERNS... ...TRENDY, BUT MEANINGLESS... NO. I'LL PASS.

RASPBERRY TORTE IN THE SHAPE OF A WITCH HAT, FLOATING IN A POOL OF APRICOT PUREÉ... SOPHISTICATED...FLASHY ...BUT NO. I CAN RESIST.

GUMMY, MASS-PRODUCED CANDY BARS FILLED WITH PRESERVATIVES AND FAKE COLOR LIKE THE ONES THAT MADE ME SICK WHEN I WAS LITTLE....
YES! YES! YES! YES!

I WANT TO DO TO WOMEN'S HEARTS WHAT THESE DO TO THEIR BRAINS.

SOME TRICK-OR-TREATERS ARE COMING. GET THE CANDY, CATHY!
I DON'T LIKE TO GET IT OUT TOO EARLY.
THEY'RE AT THE DOOR!
THERE'S PLENTY OF TIME, IRVING.

DING DONG!

TRICK OR TREAT!
YOU'RE TOO LATE.

YOU LEARN TO BE QUICK WITH CHILDREN.

BUSINESS DEALINGS REEL OUT OF CONTROL...
...SELL! NO, BUY!.. ..NO, SELL!... WAIT... HOLD ON... WAIT...
CATHY

PERSONAL RELATIONSHIPS SNAP LIKE SUSPENDERS...
...WAIT... HANG ON... I DIDN'T MEAN THAT, SWEETIE... WAIT.. ACK..

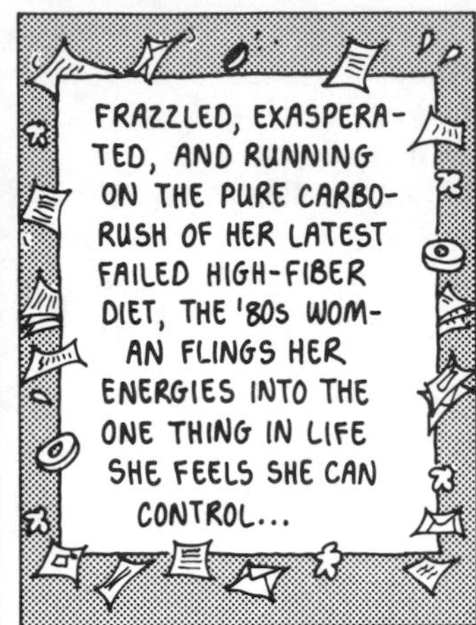
FRAZZLED, EXASPERATED, AND RUNNING ON THE PURE CARBO-RUSH OF HER LATEST FAILED HIGH-FIBER DIET, THE '80s WOMAN FLINGS HER ENERGIES INTO THE ONE THING IN LIFE SHE FEELS SHE CAN CONTROL...

...THE DESTRUCTION OF HER HAIR.
CUT IT! PERM IT! WEAVE IT!
MOUSSE

ONE DAY, IN 1982, FOR 15 MINUTES, MY HAIR WAS PERFECT.

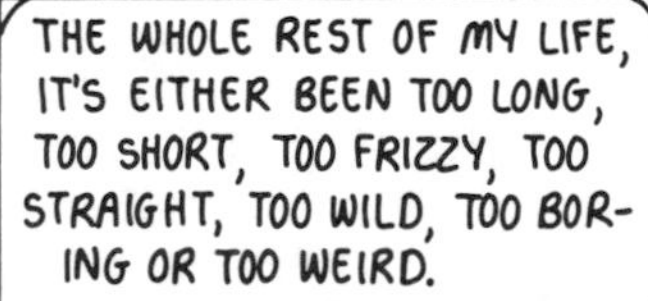
THE WHOLE REST OF MY LIFE, IT'S EITHER BEEN TOO LONG, TOO SHORT, TOO FRIZZY, TOO STRAIGHT, TOO WILD, TOO BORING OR TOO WEIRD.

YET I'VE ALWAYS VIEWED THE 15 PERFECT MINUTES AS HOW MY HAIR "NORMALLY" IS, AND THE REST OF THE TIME AS A SERIES OF LITTLE PROBLEMS THAT I SOMEHOW CAUSED BY SOMETHING I DID OR DIDN'T DO.

THINK OF THIS LESS LIKE A HAIRCUT AND MORE LIKE A DIVORCE.

WHAT DO YOU WANT DONE TO YOUR HAIR?
OH...HEE, HEE... I DON'T KNOW... WHATEVER YOU THINK BEST.
Hot Rollers

Snip.
AACK! BUTCHERY! YOU'RE COMBING IT WRONG! YOU'RE CUTTING IT WRONG!!

IT'S TOO NOISY IN HERE!! EVERYONE EITHER SHUT UP OR LEAVE THE SHOP!! AND TURN OFF THAT RADIO! I WILL NOT HAVE MUSICIANS BORN AFTER I GRADUATED FROM COLLEGE INFLUENCING THE HAIRDO I GET!!!

DID YOU HAVE A CERTAIN STYLE IN MIND?
I DON'T KNOW... ...HEE, HEE... WHATEVER YOU THINK BEST....
Hot Rollers

I WANT MY HAIR TO LOOK JUST LIKE THIS!!

THAT'S A 5'9", 110-POUND NATURAL REDHEAD WITH EMERALD EYES AND CHEEKBONES THAT ARE INSURED FOR TWO MILLION DOLLARS.

DO YOU SWEAR YOU WON'T SUE ME IF YOU DON'T WIND UP LOOKING LIKE HER IDENTICAL TWIN?
OH, HA, HA! WHAT A KIDDER! HA, HA!

COME AS CLOSE AS YOU CAN.
GET ME A CAN OF MOUSSE AND MY LAWYER.

SUE THE HAIR STYLIST!!

I'M PICKETING THE SHOP!! I'M CALLING THE OWNER!! I'M WRITING THE BETTER BUSINESS BUREAU!! I'LL HAVE HER LICENSE REVOKED! I'LL PUT HER OUT OF BUSINESS!!

SHE WILL RUE THE DAY SHE TRASHED MY LIFE FOR $65 PLUS TIP!!!
YOU GAVE HER A TIP??

I DIDN'T WANT HER TO THINK I WAS DISSATISFIED.

TELL ME MY HAIR ISN'T GOING TO STAY LIKE THIS!
NO...THE CURL WILL RELAX IN A FEW WEEKS, CATHY.

THEN IT WILL LOOK FLAT AND SCRAGGLY ON TOP SO YOU'LL GET IT LAYERED...THE LAYERS WILL MAKE YOUR GRAY HAIRS POP OUT, SO YOU'LL GET IT COLORED....

THE COLOR WILL FINISH FRYING THE ENDS, SO YOU'LL GET IT HACKED OFF...THEN IT WILL BE SHORT, DRAB AND LIFELESS, SO YOU'LL GET IT RE-PERMED AND START ALL OVER!

THIS IS ACTUALLY THE BEST YOUR HAIR WILL LOOK FOR THE NEXT 25 YEARS.
LEAVE MY HOME, CHARLENE.

WHY ARE YOU WEARING A HAT, CATHY?
HAT??...OH, YES.. AHEM...I WAS A LITTLE CHILLY...

SOMEONE'S WEARING A HAT??
DID I HEAR HAT??
HAT??
WHO HAS THE HAT?!
THERE'S A HAT IN THE OFFICE?

WHAT'S THIS??
YOU KNOW THE OLD SAYING, CATHY... WHERE THERE'S SMOKE, THERE'S FIRE...

...AND WHERE THERE'S A HAT, THERE'S A PERM.
CLAP CLAP
CLAP CLAP
CLAP CLAP
Guisewite

WHY DIDN'T YOU TALK TO ME ABOUT GETTING A PERM BEFORE YOU DID IT, CATHY??
I DIDN'T WANT TO BE INFLUENCED BY YOU, IRVING.

DOESN'T MY OPINION COUNT?
I JUST WANTED THIS TO BE MY OWN DECISION.

FOR ONCE IN MY LIFE, I WANTED TO DO SOMETHING WHERE I WASN'T CHECKING WITH YOU EVERY 10 SECONDS TO SEE IF YOU APPROVED!!

...FROM A PRISONER OF LOVE TO A PRISONER OF HAIR.
Guisewite

I HATE YOUR HAIR. THERE. DO YOU WANT ME TO SAY I LIKE IT IF I DON'T?
NO.

I JUST CAN'T BELIEVE YOU'RE SUDDENLY REJECTING ALL OF ME JUST BECAUSE OF A HAIRDO.

IF YOU'RE GOING TO JUDGE ME ON SOMETHING AS SUPERFICIAL AS HAIR AFTER ALL WE'VE BEEN THROUGH TOGETHER, JUST FORGET IT, IRVING! FORGET IT!!

CATHY, HOW DID YOU FIND THE STRENGTH TO THROW HIM OUT?!
I DIDN'T LIKE THE SHIRT HE WAS WEARING.
Guisewite

IF A MAN ISN'T INTERESTED IN A RELATIONSHIP, HE CAN JUST QUIT CALLING... IF A WOMAN ISN'T INTERESTED, SHE ALMOST ALWAYS HAS TO EXPLAIN IT WITH WORDS.

A MAN CAN JUST DISAPPEAR... A WOMAN SPENDS WEEKS TORTURING HERSELF ABOUT HOW TO REJECT HIM WITHOUT HURTING HIS FEELINGS OR DIGNITY.

THIS IS JUST ONE MORE AREA OF LIFE WHERE MEN GET TO ACCOMPLISH EXACTLY THE SAME THING IN 1/100TH OF THE TIME WE HAVE TO SPEND.... AND THEN THEY HAVE THE NERVE TO WONDER WHY WE TEND TO RUN LATE!!!
GUISEWITE

NOT TO MENTION ALL THE TIME IT TAKES TO TWIST EVERY SITUATION SO IT TURNS OUT TO BE THEIR FAULT, CATHY.
IT'S A WONDER WE EVER SLEEP, CHARLENE...

HIS ANSWERING MACHINE. PERFECT.
SLAM!

WHAT WERE YOU GOING TO SAY TO HIM?
I DON'T KNOW. PART OF ME HATES HIM, AND PART OF ME JUST WANTS TO BE WITH HIM AND MAKE EVERYTHING BETTER.

BUT I CAN'T EVEN START THE CONVERSATION IF I KEEP GETTING HIS ANSWERING MACHINE!
I KNOW, CATHY... UNREQUITED LOVE.

EVEN WORSE. UNREQUITED AMBIVALENCE.

MY BOYFRIEND ISN'T SPEAKING TO ME BECAUSE OF MY HAIR... MY OFFICE RIDICULES ME... I CAN'T STAND TO LOOK AT MYSELF...
I THINK YOUR PERM IS LOVELY, CATHY!

MOM, I DON'T WANT PHONEY COMPLIMENTS. I WANT COMPASSION.
I KNOW JUST HOW YOU FEEL. LET'S GO SHOPPING FOR A WIG.

I THOUGHT YOU LIKED IT.
WELL, YES, IT'S LOVELY...
WHY SHOULD I SHOP FOR A WIG?
ONLY IF YOU WANT THE WIG...
IF IT'S SO LOVELY, WHY WOULD I WANT A WIG?
ONE MOMENT, PLEASE...

I WAS WALKING THE LINE BETWEEN MOTHER AND FRIEND AND I FELL INTO THE CREVICE.

"CROSS MY HEART"... ...ONE MOVIE, AND SUDDENLY THE FIGHT I'VE BEEN HAVING WITH IRVING SEEMS SO PETTY.
YEAH... SAME WITH FRANKIE AND ME, CATHY.
Cross My Heart
STARRING MARTIN SHORT

I MEAN, MAYBE MEN ARE JUST AS INSECURE AS WE ARE.
MEN GO THROUGH THE EXACT SAME THINGS... THEY FEEL JUST THE SAME...

I HAVE TO TALK TO HIM, CHARLENE.
YEAH, I KNOW WHAT YOU MEAN...

GET ME THE PHONE NUMBER FOR MARTIN SHORT!!
GET IN LINE.
PHONE

I'M SORRY I WAS SO HARD ON YOU ABOUT YOUR NEW HAIRDO, CATHY.
YOU DESERTED ME WHEN I NEEDED YOU MOST, IRVING.

I'M SORRY. I WAS WRONG.
SOMETIMES A PERSON HAS TO BE THERE JUST BECAUSE THE OTHER PERSON NEEDS IT... YOU HAVE TO PUT YOUR FEELINGS ASIDE AND JUST BE THERE FOR SUPPORT!!

I KNOW...AND THAT'S WHY I KNOW YOU'LL BE THERE FOR ME WHEN MY PARENTS VISIT THIS WEEK.

EVERY TIME I TAKE COMMAND, I LEAD MY ARMY OVER THE CLIFF.
Guisewite

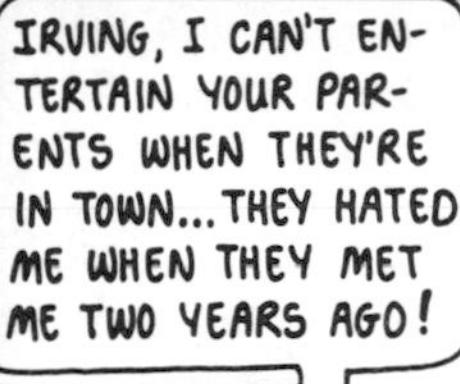

IRVING, I CAN'T ENTERTAIN YOUR PARENTS WHEN THEY'RE IN TOWN...THEY HATED ME WHEN THEY MET ME TWO YEARS AGO!
THEY DIDN'T HATE YOU, CATHY.

AND NOW LOOK AT ME... I GAINED SIX POUNDS OVER HALLOWEEN... MY PERM IS A DISASTER... MY FACE HAS BROKEN OUT FROM STRESS... I BIT OFF ALL MY NAILS BECAUSE OF THE FAT, THE PERM AND THE FACE... ..AND YOU AND I HAVE BARELY BEEN SPEAKING TO EACH OTHER!

OK. MAYBE WE SHOULD JUST SKIP IT.

WHAT'S THE MATTER?? AREN'T YOU PROUD OF ME?!
Guisewite

IRVING, BEFORE YOUR MOTHER COMES HERE, I NEED TO KNOW WHAT YOU'VE TOLD HER ABOUT US LATELY.
WHAT DO YOU MEAN, CATHY?

WHAT DO YOU SAY IS GOING ON WITH US?... WHAT DOES SHE THINK ABOUT WHAT YOU THINK ABOUT ME?... WAS SHE UPSET ABOUT OUR FIGHT?... DID SHE COACH YOU ON WHAT TO SAY TO ME TONIGHT?...

YOU'RE KIDDING, RIGHT?? YOU DON'T DO THAT WITH YOUR MOTHER, DO YOU?
ME?? HA, HA.. ...NO! ME?? ...MOM HAS NO IDEA WHAT'S GOING ON WITH ME! HA, HA!

DON'T CALL CATHY YET, DEAR. ROUND TWO SHOULD JUST BE BEGINNING.

Guisewite

THE BOYFRIEND'S PARENTS' ANNUAL VISIT APPROACHES, AND A LIFETIME OF CAREFULLY NUR-TURED HOMEMAKING SKILLS SNAP INTO ACTION.

CALLING ON EVERY CREATIVE INSTINCT...EVERY "ELEGANT HOSTESS" ARTICLE...EVERY HOUR OF WATCHING HER MOTH-ER EFFORTLESSLY WHIP TO-GETHER HORS D'OEUVRES....

...THE '80s WOMAN EMERGES. REFINED...GRACIOUS...PROUD...

CATHY, IT'S IRVING AND MY PARENTS.
DING DONG!
WAIT ONE SECOND... JUST A SEC...

WE'RE FREEZING OUT HERE.
COMING... ONE SEC... JUST A SEC...

NEVER MIND. I CAN JUST LET US IN WITH MY KEY....
NO! DO NOT SAY YOU HAVE A....

...HI.
TOO LATE. YOUR CAN OF WORMS HAS ALREADY BEEN OPENED.

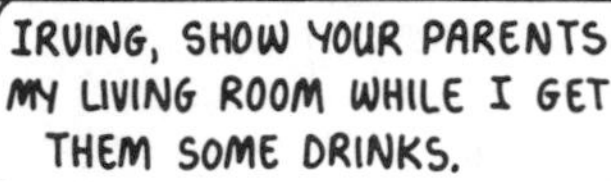
IRVING, SHOW YOUR PARENTS MY LIVING ROOM WHILE I GET THEM SOME DRINKS.

I HAVE MIXED DRINKS, WINE, DIET SOFT DRINKS, REGULAR SOFT DRINKS, LEMONADE, BEER, 12 KINDS OF COFFEE, 17 KINDS OF TEA, 23 KINDS OF BOTTLED WATER AND 9 TYPES OF JUICE.
I'LL HAVE HAWAIIAN PUNCH.

...AHAH! AND HAWAIIAN PUNCH!!

SHE PASSED THE PUNCH TEST, BUT FLUNKED THE HUMILITY TEST.

CATHY BOUGHT THIS CONDOMINIUM A FEW MONTHS AGO, MOM AND DAD. ISN'T IT GREAT?
YOUR PLACE IS THIS NICE, IRVING.

WELL, SURE, BUT PEOPLE EXPECT A MAN OUR AGE TO BE DOING WELL.

WHEN A WOMAN HAS DEVOTED HERSELF TO HER CAREER ENOUGH TO HAVE ACHIEVED THIS MUCH, IT MEANS SOMETHING A LITTLE MORE SIGNIFICANT!!

SHE CAN'T COOK.

CATHY DECORATED THIS PLACE BY HERSELF.
SHE'S LUCKY SHE'S YOUNG ENOUGH TO NOT GET BACK PROBLEMS FROM A SOFA THIS SQUISHY.

OH... WAIT... MAYBE YOU'D BE MORE COMFORTABLE IN A WOODEN CHAIR.
YOU'RE LUCKY YOUR SKIN IS STILL STRONG ENOUGH TO NOT GET SPLINTERS FROM A WOODEN CHAIR.

...HERE. I HAVE A METAL STOOL... HERE'S A NICE, FIRM LOVESEAT... HERE'S A BENCH... HERE'S AN OTTOMAN... HERE'S A RECLINER....

COMFORTABLE, MOTHER?
IT COULD BE A NICE ROOM IF IT WEREN'T SO CLUTTERED.

IRVING, DON'T PUT YOUR GLASS ON THE TABLE. YOU'LL MAKE A SPOT.
IF HE DOESN'T KNOW BY NOW, HE ISN'T GOING TO LEARN.

DON'T SET IT ON YOUR LEG. YOUR PANT KNEE WILL SHRINK.
THEY'RE HIS PANTS. LET HIM SHRINK THEM IF HE WANTS.

DON'T DRINK SO FAST. YOU'LL GET HICCUPS.
MAYBE HE WANTS HICCUPS.

HERE, IRVING, WHY DON'T YOU USE THIS COASTER?
CAN YOU BELIEVE IT ?? SHE'S PICKING ON OUR SON!!

YOUR MOTHER HATES ME, IRVING!
NO, SHE DOESN'T.

SHE HATES MY HOUSE. SHE HATES MY FURNITURE. SHE HATES MY FACE!
YOU'RE JUST NOT USED TO HOW SHE ACTS.

REALLY?
TRUST ME, CATHY...
THERE YOU ARE, MY HANDSOME GENIUS BABY!!

...SHE'S JUST NOT THE DEMONSTRATIVE TYPE.

UM...MAYBE WE SHOULD TALK ABOUT WHAT HAPPENED YESTERDAY SO IT WON'T TURN INTO SOME HUGE UNSPOKEN PROBLEM, IRVING.
LET'S NOT WORRY ABOUT IT TONIGHT, CATHY.

WHEW! I DIDN'T WANT TO TALK ABOUT IT... I JUST THOUGHT YOU MIGHT WANT TO TALK ABOUT IT.
BLEAH. I DON'T WANT TO TALK ABOUT IT.

PERFECT! WE WON'T TALK ABOUT IT!
COUPLES LIKE US DON'T HAVE TO TALK ABOUT EVERY LITTLE THING...WE UNDERSTAND THE BIG PICTURE!

WHY RUIN THE MOMENT WHEN YOU CAN TRASH THE NEXT SIX MONTHS?
Guisewite

IT WAS NICE OF YOUR MOTHER TO INVITE MY PARENTS FOR BRUNCH, CATHY, BUT....
WE ACCEPT.

YOU SAID BRUNCH GIVES YOU A RASH, MOM.
I CHANGED MY MIND.
YOU SAID EATING SCRAMBLED EGGS WITH STRANGERS MADE YOU NAUSEOUS.
I EXAGGERATED.

IRVING MAKES ME SOUND LIKE SUCH AN OGRE. OF COURSE WE'D LOVE TO MEET YOUR PARENTS!
GREAT...

I WANT TO SEE IF THAT HAIR OF HERS RUNS IN THE GENE POOL OR WAS JUST A FREAK OF NATURE.

HOW NICE THAT IRVING'S PARENTS COULD COME FOR BRUNCH. HOW'D IT GO WITH THEM AT YOUR HOUSE?
HORRIBLE, MOM. EVERY SINGLE THING THAT COULD GO WRONG WENT WRONG.

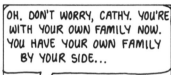

OH, DON'T WORRY, CATHY. YOU'RE WITH YOUR OWN FAMILY NOW. YOU HAVE YOUR OWN FAMILY BY YOUR SIDE...

CALL THE PARAMEDICS! I THINK I'VE BEEN POISONED!!
YOU'RE SQUASHING MY FAVORITE CHAIR!!
AACK! THERE'S A BEETLE ON THE WALL!

...AND WE'LL BE RIGHT DOWN THERE IN THE SEWER WITH YOU.
Guisewite

CATHY, YOU'VE HARDLY TOUCHED YOUR EGGS.
MOM...
IRVING, YOU'RE USING YOUR DESSERT FORK ON THE SAUSAGE.
MOM...

YOU DON'T NEED ANOTHER ROLL.
YOUR SLEEVE IS IN YOUR JUICE.
HAVE ANOTHER ROLL.
EAT YOUR FRUIT. YOU NEED THE ROUGHAGE.
YOU'RE BETTER OFF WITH A ROLL THAN ALL THOSE POTATOES.

MOM!!

I WIN.
YOU HAD A HEAD START.
Guisewite

SO... HERE WE ALL ARE...
SO...
SO...
SO...
SO...
SO...

IRVING AND IRVING'S PARENTS... CATHY AND CATHY'S PARENTS...

WE'VE ALL HAD A CHANCE TO GET TO KNOW ONE ANOTHER AND... WELL... AS FUN AS IT WOULD BE TO GO ON SHRIEKING AT EACH OTHER ALL DAY, I GUESS WE'RE ALL WONDERING IF THE YOUNG COUPLE HAS ANY PLANS FOR THE FUTURE....

WE PLAN TO BREAK UP AS SOON AS BRUNCH IS OVER.
SECOND!
MOTION CARRIED!
GUISEWITE

PLEASE LOOK US UP WHENEVER YOU'RE IN TOWN!
WE WILL! AND WE HOPE YOU DO THE SAME!

HOW COULD YOU SAY THAT, MOM?? THIS WAS THE WORST EVENT OF OUR LIVES!!
WE HAD GREAT FUN!

AWKWARD SILENCES... HYSTERICAL OUTBURSTS... EVERY NEUROSIS GONE BERSERK...
THINGS JUST SEEM DIFFERENT AT OUR AGE, CATHY.

THIS IS AS CLOSE AS WE GET TO THE THRILL OF DATING.
GUISEWITE

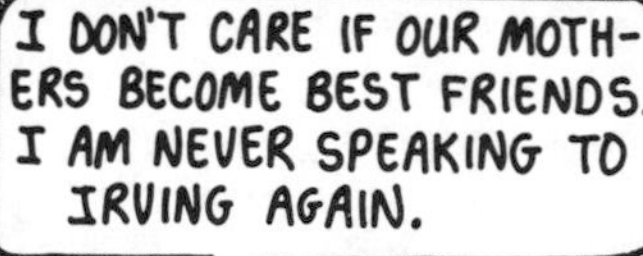
I DON'T CARE IF OUR MOTHERS BECOME BEST FRIENDS. I AM NEVER SPEAKING TO IRVING AGAIN.

NO MORE CALLS. NO MORE VISITS. NO MORE DATES. LET HIM BEG. IT'S TOO LATE!

IT'S OVER! IT'S FINISHED! IT'S HISTORY! KAPUT!!
WHAT ARE YOU GOING TO DO TONIGHT?

GO SHOPPING FOR HIS CHRISTMAS PRESENT.
GUISEWITE

...EVEN THE FRIENDS WE NEVER SPEAK TO CONTINUE TO INSPIRE HOW WE LIVE.

CARDS

ADDRESS BOOK

Guisewite

OH, THIS WILL MAKE SUCH A SPECIAL, BEAUTIFUL GIFT!
YES... WON'T IT?...

YOU MUST BE A VERY THOUGHTFUL PERSON TO GIVE A GIFT THIS NICE!
YES... AHEM... THANK YOU...
SUCH CARING... SUCH A SACRIFICE...
YES, WELL...

BERNIE, LOOK WHAT THIS DEAR WOMAN IS GIV....
IT'S FOR ME, OK?? I'M BUYING IT FOR MYSELF. JUST STUFF IT IN THE BAG. IT'S FOR ME!!

WHY JUST GET A SALE WHEN YOU CAN GO FOR A CONFESSION?

DIDN'T I READ IN THE PAPER THAT YOUR OLD FRIEND JEANNE GOT...
MARRIED. YES, MOM. SHE'S MARRIED.
CARDS

AND I READ THAT SUE IS...
MARRIED.
AND BETH?
MARRIED.
BECKY?
MARRIED.
JOANN?
MARRIED, PROMOTED, PREGNANT.

WELL, THAT PRETTY MUCH WRAPS UP YOUR WHOLE GRADUATING CLASS EXCEPT YOU, DOESN'T IT, SWEETIE?
AAUGH!
CARDS

VERBAL CLIPPINGS: ALL OF THE AGGRAVATION, NONE OF THE EVIDENCE.
CARDS

CATALOGS FILLED WITH PERFECT CHRISTMAS PRESENTS THAT I WAS TOO LAZY TO SPEND 15 SECONDS ORDERING...
TO DO!
1000 GIFTS
FOR HIM

GIFTS I STARTED TO HANDMAKE IN 1979 THAT I SWORE I'D FINISH THIS YEAR...MAGAZINES FILLED WITH ABANDONED HOLIDAY ENTERTAINMENT FANTASIES....

CHRISTMAS CARDS I GOT LAST YEAR THAT I STILL OWE LETTERS TO...

WE HAVE TO GO TO THE MALL. IT'S TOO CROWDED IN MY HOUSE.

AACK!! SHOP! WRAP! BAKE! WRITE!! NO TIME! NO TIME!! WHY DON'T YOU HUG ME?! DON'T TOUCH ME, I'M TOO FAT! AACK!! AACK!!

AACK!

HOW DO YOU AND IRVING EXPECT TO KEEP THINGS GOING IF ONE OF YOU IS ALWAYS WORKING LATE, CATHY ?
THIS HAPPENS TO WORK PERFECTLY, MOM.

IT'S NEVER BORING, NEVER MUNDANE, NEVER THE SAME OLD RUT.

WHEN IRVING AND I FINALLY GET TO SEE EACH OTHER AFTER WHOLE WEEKS OF BEING APART, WE HAVE THAT RARE SOMETHING THAT FEW COUPLES EVER GET TO EXPERIENCE....

...TOTAL WEIRDNESS.
SO...UM, I DON'T KNOW...WHAT'S NEW WITH YOU ?....
Guisewite

HOW ABOUT THIS $400 JACKET FOR YOUR BOY-FRIEND?
NO. TOO EXPENSIVE. ..I DON'T WANT HIM TO FEEL PRESSURED BY THE FACT THAT I'D SPEND THAT MUCH ON HIM.

HOW ABOUT THIS $5.00 KEYCASE?
NO. TOO CHEAP. I DON'T WANT HIM TO FEEL THAT'S ALL HE'S WORTH TO ME.

HOW ABOUT THIS TOTALLY BLAND SWEATER? TOO NICE TO BE IN-SULTING, BUT TOO TACKY TO BE A THREAT?
YES! HE'D BE COMFORT-ABLE WITH THAT! NO PRESSURE... NO STATE-MENT...YES!

FOR THE ONE I LOVE: THE GIFT OF MEDIOCRITY.
Guisewite

MY MOTHER SPENDS THE HOLIDAYS GRILLING ME ABOUT MY LOVE LIFE. IT MAKES ME CRAZY.
MY MOTHER PICKS APART ALL MY FRIENDS AND THEN ASKS WHY I DON'T BRING THEM HOME WITH ME.

HAH! MINE FORCES ME TO LOOK AT PIC-TURES OF MY EX-FRIENDS' CHILDREN AT THEIR VIOLIN RECITALS!
MINE STUFFS ME WITH FOOD AND THEN COM-MENTS THAT I'M PUTTING ON WEIGHT!

HAH! WELL, MY MOTHER DOESN'T EVEN HAVE TO SPEAK! MY MOTHER CAN REDUCE ME TO A 3-YEAR-OLD IN 15 SEC-ONDS JUST BY LOOKING AT ME!!
HMPH.

MY MOM...AFTER ALL THESE YEARS, NO OTHER MOTHER EVEN COMES CLOSE.
Guisewite

MY MOTHER'S GOING TO MAKE ME NUTS WHEN I GO HOME FOR CHRISTMAS, CATHY.
YOU JUST CAN'T GIVE IN TO IT, CHARLENE.

OUR PARENTS AREN'T GOING TO BE WITH US FOREVER... IF WE DON'T RELAX AND APPRE-CIATE THEM NOW, WE'LL REGRET IT THE REST OF OUR LIVES.
RING

NO, I DO NOT KNOW WHAT TIME I'M AR-RIVING YET, MOTHER!!

WHAT'S ALL THE COMMO-TION?
THE ANNUAL HOLIDAY SELF-RIGHTEOUS SPEECH EXCHANGE.
Guisewite

— CHRISTMAS WEEK, 1987 — NERVES ARE FRAYED, EMOTIONS EXHAUSTED. EXPECTATIONS WHIP AROUND LIKE LITTLE BLIZZARDS.

DESPERATE FOR CONNECTION AND REASSURANCE, PEOPLE TURN WITH A WHOLE NEW PASSION TO THEIR MOST SOLID SOURCE OF SECURITY.....

MEN TO MONDAY NIGHT FOOTBALL. WOMEN TO THE THERAPIST.

...COFFEE CUP! YES! I COULD HAVE GOTTEN IRVING A COFFEE CUP FOR CHRISTMAS!!
PINKLEY

...WAIT! YOU HAVE PAPER! MEN LOVE PAPER! WHY DIDN'T I THINK OF PAPER??...AND A NECKTIE! I'LL GIVE YOU $10 FOR YOUR NECKTIE! $15 FOR THE NECKTIE AND SOCKS!!

ANYTHING! I'LL BUY ANYTHING ANYONE IN THIS COMPANY HAS!!!

TIME TO CLOSE THE OFFICE FOR THE HOLIDAYS, MR. PINKLEY.
ARE YOU KIDDING? THIS IS WHEN I DO SOME OF MY BEST BUSINESS.

FORTY-EIGHT HOURS BEFORE I GO HOME FOR CHRISTMAS, I START EATING. I ANTICIPATE AGGRAVATION, SO I EAT.

I OUTGROW MY CLOTHES...
I BITE MY NAILS...
I GIVE MYSELF WRINKLES...
I TURN INTO A GROUCH...

FORTY-EIGHT HOURS BEFORE FACING THE ONE PERSON WHOSE APPROVAL IS MOST IMPORTANT TO ME, I FLING MYSELF INTO TOTAL SELF-DESTRUCT.

ALL READY TO COME HOME FOR CHRISTMAS, SWEETIE?
ALMOST, MOM. I JUST HAVE TO FINISH OFF MY HAIR.

THE MOTHER READIES THE NEST...
I WANT EVERYTHING TO BE PERFECT FOR WHEN CATHY COMES HOME!

THE YOUNG FAMILY SNUGGLES INTO A COCOON...
A COZY LITTLE CHRISTMAS WITH JUST THE THREE OF US!

YA HA! WALK THROUGH THAT DOOR DURING THE HOLIDAYS, IRVING, AND YOU'RE NOT ESCAPING UNTIL YOU MAKE SOME DECISION ABOUT OUR RELATIONSHIP!!

THE SINGLE WOMAN SETS UP A ROACH MOTEL.

IS THE VIDEOTAPE IN??
YES! LOOK! THERE WE ALL ARE ON THE TUBE! MERRY CHRISTMAS!!

THERE WE ARE OPENING THE GIFTS! REMEMBER HOW CATHY RIPPED THAT ONE OPEN?! HA, HA!
REMEMBER HOW DAD ALMOST SPILLED HIS COFFEE ON THE ROBINSONS' FRUITCAKE?! WHAT A RIOT!

OH, WHAT A TIME! WHAT MEMORIES!!
THAT WAS ONLY 15 MINUTES AGO, MOM AND DAD.

WE LOOKED SO YOUNG!!

NOW HERE'S A SIGHT THAT WARMS A MOTHER'S HEART!

ONE DAY AFTER CHRISTMAS, AND HERE YOU ARE, WORKING AWAY!

AND TO THINK THE EXAMPLE I'VE SET THROUGH THE YEARS HAS FINALLY HAD AN IMPACT!
CATHY'S ACTUALLY STARTED HER THANK-YOU NOTES?

DON'T BE RIDICULOUS. SHE'S STARTED HER CHRISTMAS CARDS!

I SHOULD BE BACK AT THE OFFICE TODAY, MOM.
I KNOW, SWEETIE... BUT IF YOU GO TODAY, YOU'LL BE TOO GUILT-RIDDEN THINKING THAT I'M JUST SITTING HERE WEEPING WITH YOUR FATHER.

FINE. I'LL STAY.
OH, BUT YOU'RE SO BUSY. YOU SHOULD GO.
FINE. I'LL GO.
WE LOOKED FORWARD TO THIS TIME ALL YEAR.
FINE. I'LL STAY.
NO. IT'S TIME FOR YOU TO GO.

I'M STAYING, MOM!
NO. GO. I WANT YOU TO GO.
I WANT TO STAY!
NO. GO. YOU SHOULD GO.
PLEASE LET ME STAY!
NO! GO! YOU MUST GO!

JUST CALL US TWO GIRLS WHO DON'T KNOW HOW TO LET THE PARTY END.

WHO'S THAT, CATHY?
I DON'T KNOW.
ADDRESSES

IF YOU DON'T KNOW WHO IT IS, WHY ARE YOU TRANSFERRING HER INTO YOUR NEW ADDRESS BOOK?
IT WOULD SEEM INSULTING TO JUST THROW HER OUT.

IF SHE WAS IMPORTANT ENOUGH TO ME ONCE TO BE PUT IN MY ADDRESS BOOK, THEN SHE DESERVES TO **STAY** IN MY ADDRESS BOOK!

I NEVER LOSE SIGHT OF MY FRIENDSHIPS... I JUST FORGET WHO THE PEOPLE ARE.

ADDRESSES
Addresses

THE NEKERVISES WILL BE SO DISAPPOINTED IF THEY DON'T GET TO SEE YOU DURING THE HOLIDAYS, CATHY.

MOM, THE NEKERVISES HAVE 45 RELATIVES OF THEIR OWN IN TOWN.

THEY'LL BE DISAPPOINTED... THEIR CHILDREN WILL BE DISAPPOINTED... THE GRANDCHILDREN WILL BE DISAPPOINTED...

FLO'S BEEN TALKING TO THEM ABOUT YOUR VISIT ALL WEEK!

CATHY WILL BE SO DISAPPOINTED IF SHE DOESN'T GET TO SEE YOU FOR THE HOLIDAYS.

NEW YEAR'S EVE, 1987... A MORE TRANQUIL FEELING IS IN THE AIR AS MILLIONS OF AMERICANS SETTLE INTO A DECADE-LONG TREND TOWARD MONOGAMY...

FROM THE HIGH-RISES IN NEW YORK TO THE BEACH HOUSES IN HAWAII, WOMEN ARE DISCOVERING THE COZY SECURITY OF ENDING THE YEAR WITH THE SAME MAN WITH WHOM THEY BEGAN IT...

CYBILL AND BRUCE... DEMI AND BRUCE... ALEX AND JOHNNY... JILLY AND TOM... PHYLICIA AND AHMAD... GEENA AND JEFF... CAITLIN AND SONNY... JENNA AND RAY...

CATHY AND ORVILLE REDENBACHER.
diet
Guisewite

WHY?
WHY, WHY, WHY?
diet
diet

WHY DID I THINK TWO MINUTES WITH A CHOCOLATE MOUSSE WAS WORTH IT?? WHY DID I HAVE TO HAVE THAT ONE LAST ICE CREAM BALL?? WHY DID I NEED FOUR PIECES OF CHEESECAKE?!

diet
diet

diet
diet
Guisewite

WHY DIDN'T I EAT MORE YESTERDAY WHEN I HAD THE CHANCE??
diet
diet

WELL, THAT DOES IT FOR 1987....
CATH

...WAIT A MINUTE. THERE WAS AN AREA CODE MAP IN THAT CALENDAR?? I NEVER SAW THE AREA CODE MAP!

1987

...WHAT'S THIS?? A ZODIAC CHART??... A METRIC CONVERSION TABLE??... I SPENT 365 DAYS WITH THIS CALENDAR AND I DIDN'T NOTICE IT HAD A ZIP CODE DIRECTORY!??

1987

YOU NEVER REALLY GET TO KNOW SOMEONE UNTIL YOU BREAK UP.
CATH
Guisewite

THINGS HAVE BEEN HORRIBLE WITH FRANKIE.
THINGS HAVE BEEN GREAT WITH IRVING.

HE ALWAYS THINKS HE'S RIGHT. HE WON'T LISTEN TO ME!
IRVING USUALLY THINKS HE'S RIGHT, BUT HE SORT OF LISTENS...

HE CRITICIZES ME AND THEN SAYS I HAVE NO CONFIDENCE!
IRVING DOES THAT, TOO.
JUST WHEN I'M READY TO CONFRONT HIM, HE WORKS UNTIL MIDNIGHT AND TURNS OFF HIS ANSWERING MACHINE!
IRVING DOES THAT, TOO! I HATE THAT!!

READY TO ORDER?
NO, BUT THE CRISIS TRANSFER IS ALMOST COMPLETE.

A FRUITCAKE FROM A FRIEND IN MISSOURI.
POINK!

RIP!
A GIFT BASKET OF COOKIES FROM BELGIUM.
POP!
A DOZEN WHITE CHOCOLATE SANTA CLAUSES FROM BALTIMORE...

GO AWAY! CHRISTMAS IS OVER! NEW YEAR'S IS FINISHED!! I HAVE A LIFE TO GET BACK TO AND I HAVE NO TIME TO DEAL WITH YOU!!

I'LL BE A LITTLE LATE TODAY, MR. PINKLEY. I CAN'T GET MY HOLIDAY COMPANY TO LEAVE.
Guisewite

SO, WHAT MIRACLE DIET IS IT GOING TO BE THIS YEAR, CATHY?
MIRACLE DIETS ARE OUT, CHARLENE. THIS YEAR I'M BEGINNING MY "FOOD PROGRAM FOR LIFE"!

RATHER THAN DEPRIVE MYSELF OF WHOLE CATEGORIES OF FOOD, I WILL LEARN TO EAT ALL FOOD IN MODERATION.

SEE? IF THE FOOD'S AROUND ME ALL THE TIME, I LEARN I CAN EAT ONE MUFFIN WITHOUT EATING THE WHOLE BOX... I CAN HAVE A TASTE OF PIE WITHOUT EATING THE WHOLE THING... I CAN HAVE ONE CHOCOLATE WITHOUT.....
ICE CREAM

SO, WHAT MIRACLE DIET IS IT GOING TO BE THIS YEAR, CATHY?
WHAT HAVE YOU HEARD OF?
CHOCOLATE
ICE CREAM
Guisewite

I'VE LOST MY INCENTIVE, MY MOMENTUM AND MY MOTIVATION.
DIET DIARY 1986
DIET DIARY 1976

I'VE LOST MY DRIVE, MY DIRECTION, MY WILLPOWER, MY RESOLVE, MY STAMINA, MY DETERMINATION, MY SENSE OF HUMOR AND MY DIGNITY.

AFTER 14 YEARS OF DIETING, THERE ARE ONLY TWO THINGS I'VE NEVER LOST.
DIET DIARY 1982

HOPE AND WEIGHT.
Guisewite

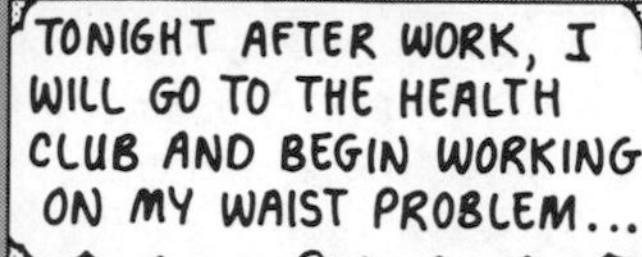
TONIGHT AFTER WORK, I WILL GO TO THE HEALTH CLUB AND BEGIN WORKING ON MY WAIST PROBLEM...

WHEN I SEE PROGRESS ON THE WAIST, I'LL FOCUS ON THE THIGH PROBLEM AND REAR PROBLEM...

...WHICH WILL BE IMMEDIATELY FOLLOWED BY INTENSE PROGRAMS FOR THE ARM PROBLEM, CALF PROBLEM AND DOUBLE CHIN PROBLEM!!
ONE WEEK INTO THE NEW YEAR: MY DESK IS STILL A MESS, BUT MY FAT IS BETTER ORGANIZED.

HOW MUCH IS IT TO RENEW MY HEALTH CLUB MEMBERSHIP?
IF YOU RENEW TODAY, THE FEE IS $325.
1988 RENEWAL SPECIAL
HEALTH CLUB
THAT INCLUDES A SESSION WITH A TRAINER WHO WILL COMPARE ALL CURRENT MEASUREMENTS AGAINST LAST YEAR AT THIS TIME!
COMPARE ALL MEASUREMENTS?

PLUS, HE'LL CHECK THE PROGRESS YOU'VE MADE ON EACH MACHINE AND WILL DESIGN AN UPDATED PROGRAM BASED ON YOUR ACHIEVEMENTS!!
HOW MUCH TO RENEW AND PRETEND YOU NEVER SAW ME BEFORE?

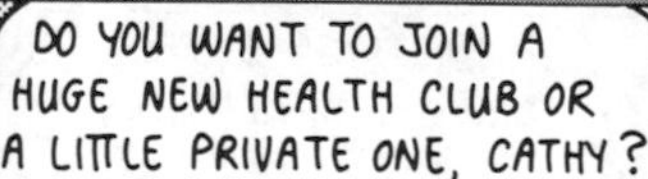
DO YOU WANT TO JOIN A HUGE NEW HEALTH CLUB OR A LITTLE PRIVATE ONE, CATHY?

HEALTH CLUB GUIDE
HEALTH CLUB GUIDE

I JUST WANT TO FIND A PLACE WHERE THERE ARE NOT ONLY ENOUGH THIN PEOPLE TO INSPIRE ME, BUT ENOUGH OVERWEIGHT PEOPLE SO I'M NOT TOTALLY DISCOURAGED.

WHEN YOU'RE SERIOUS ABOUT FITNESS, SIZE DOESN'T MATTER, CHARLENE.
HEALTH CLUB GUIDE

ALL THAT COUNTS IS FAT-MUSCLE RATIO.
HEALTH CLUB GUIDE
HEALTH CLUB GUIDE

WE WILL MEET FOR AEROBICS EVERY DAY AT 6:30A.M. AND GO RUNNING AFTER WORK!
YES!

WE WILL HAVE WEEKLY WEIGH-INS, MONITOR EACH OTHER'S DIET DIARIES AND PAY A $5.00 FINE FOR EACH CALORIE OVER 1,200!
WE'LL HAVE BIWEEKLY PURSE INSPECTIONS AND INSTALL DIET BUDDY HOTLINES ON OUR PHONES!

YES!

WE WILL NEVER SPEAK TO EACH OTHER AGAIN.
Guisewite

I DO AEROBICS, SLIMNASTICS AND JAZZERCISE.... NOTHING.

I RUN, ROW, SWIM, JUMP ROPE, AND WORK OUT ON THE MACHINES.... NOTHING.

I GLANCE AT A BLUEBERRY MUFFIN. I GAIN TWO POUNDS.
POINK!
POINK!

HOW AM I SUPPOSED TO STAY COMMITTED TO A LONG-TERM RELATIONSHIP WHEN ONE INNOCENT FLIRTATION STILL HAS THIS MUCH IMPACT?
diet
Guisewite

YOU'LL DIE OF HEAT IN THAT BIG SWEATSHIRT, CATHY.
OH, I DON'T MIND GETTING A LITTLE WARM.
AEROBICS

YOU CAN PUT YOUR SWEATSHIRT IN THE CORNER IF YOU GET TOO HOT.
THANKS BUT I, UM, LIKE TO KEEP IT WITH ME.

YOU'RE NOT GOING TO LOOK ANY WORSE IN YOUR LEOTARD THAN THE REST OF US, CATHY.
I'M COMFORTABLE. REALLY. I'M JUST FINE.

SOMETIMES I FEEL LIKE A MOTHER HEN GUARDING HER FAT.
Guisewite

I SAID "NO," CHARLENE!
YOU SAID "NO"?

"NO" TO AN APPLE TURNOVER... "NO" TO A CHOCOLATE ÉCLAIR... "NO" TO A FUDGE TORTE... "NO" TO RASPBERRY CRÊPES... "NO" TO FETTUCINI ALFREDO... "NO" TO FRENCH FRIES... "NO" TO A MILK SHAKE... "NO" TO A BAG OF DORITOS...

I HAD A PAN OF LASAGNA TWO INCHES FROM MY MOUTH, AND I SAID "NO!"!!

BRAVO, CATHY! WHAT A WEEK!
THAT WAS ON THE WAY TO WORK.
Guisewite

ONE BITE OF PIE AT A RESTAURANT, AND I CAN JUST LEAVE THE REST. I'M IN TOTAL CONTROL.

ONE BITE OF PIE AT A PARTY AND I CAN JUST LEAVE THE REST. I'M IN TOTAL CONTROL.

ONE BITE OF PIE AT HOME AND I CAN JUST....UH-OH...

HOW'D THE PIE TEST GO, CATHY?
I'M READY TO DATE ONE, BUT I'M NOT READY TO LIVE WITH ONE.
Guisewite

YOU PAID $500 TO JOIN ANOTHER HEALTH CLUB, CATHY?
I'M DESPERATE, MOM.

LOOK AT THIS... I HAVE BUSINESS CLOTHES FOR THE SKINNY ME, THE MEDIUM ME, AND THE LARGE ME.... DRESSY CLOTHES FOR THE EMACIATED ME AND THE PLUMP ME.... CASUAL CLOTHES FOR THE IN-BETWEEN FAT AND MEDIUM ME... BLUE JEANS FOR SIX DIFFERENT ME'S, INCLUDING ONE I ONLY SAW FOR AN HOUR IN 1984.

AND NOW YOU SPENT ANOTHER $500 ON STILL ANOTHER PROGRAM??

WHEN YOU COUNT HOW MANY OF ME ARE INVOLVED, IT ONLY COMES DOWN TO $17.50 A PERSON.
Guisewite

THERE ARE SOME GREAT CLASSES STARTING, CATHY.
NO, THANKS. A PERSON HAS TO LEAVE TIME IN HER LIFE FOR A RELATIONSHIP IF SHE WANTS ONE, CHARLENE.
ADULT ED

NO MORE CLASSES... NO MORE REGULAR OBLIGATIONS WITH GIRLFRIENDS... NO MORE HUGE WORK LOADS...

ADULT

I'M SACRIFICING WHATEVER IT TAKES TO ALLOW TIME FOR THE CAREFUL NURTURING OF A SOLID, LOVING RELATIONSHIP!

NOW ALL I NEED IS A DATE.
Guisewite

THE OFFICE IS CRAZY TODAY, CATHY.
OUR MOVIE DATE IS OFF...
CATHY

I MIGHT HAVE TO STAY A FEW MINUTES LATE.
DINNER IS CANCELED...
CATHY

I'LL PROBABLY BE PRETTY TIRED, BUT I'LL GIVE YOU A CALL WHEN I GET HOME.
ALL POSSIBILITY OF PHYSICAL CONTACT IS OUT FOR TONIGHT...

I DON'T UNDERSTAND THE LANGUAGE OF LOVE, BUT THE LANGUAGE OF CANCELLATION IS LIKE MY NATIVE TONGUE.
Guisewite
CAT

7:00... IRVING'S RUNNING LATE. THE HOUSE IS PERFECT. I'LL JUST CHANGE CLOTHES.
8

8:30... HE'S STILL RUNNING LATE... CHANGE CLOTHES THREE MORE TIMES... RE-DO MAKEUP ... EXPERIMENT WITH HAIR ORNAMENTS... FIX SNACK...

9:45... HE'S STILL RUNNING LATE... CHANGE CLOTHES FOUR TIMES... ALTER JACKET... ALTER PANTS... REARRANGE FURNITURE... HUNT FOR ROMANTIC MUSIC... RE-DO MANICURE..... ALTER SKIRT... RE-WASH HAIR...

CATHY, I KNOW IT'S ALMOST 11:00, BUT I'M FINALLY HERE.
I'M NOT READY YET.
8
SEWING KI
Guisewite

YOU WORK LATE FOUR NIGHTS A WEEK AND THEN EXPECT ME TO BE THERE THE ONE NIGHT YOU GET HOME AT A NORMAL TIME.
I DON'T EXPECT YOU TO BE THERE.

WELL, IF I'M NOT THERE, WE WON'T SEE EACH OTHER.
WE'LL SEE EACH OTHER ON THE NIGHTS WE'RE BOTH FREE.

IRVING, THERE'D NEVER **BE** A NIGHT WE WERE BOTH FREE IF I DIDN'T KEEP MY SCHEDULE OPEN TO ACCOMMODATE YOURS!!
DON'T TELL ME ALL THE TIMES WE'VE SEEN EACH OTHER YOU'VE JUST HELD THE NIGHT OPEN "JUST IN CASE"...

THAT WOULD BE PATHETIC, CATHY!!
JUST LIKE THE GOOD OLD DAYS... NO RELATIONSHIP IF I DON'T DO IT. NO RESPECT IF I DO...

IRVING, YOU HAVE TO WATCH "THIRTYSOMETHING" WITH ME... THIS IS EVERYTHING I WANT FOR OUR RELATIONSHIP.
THEY'RE HAVING A FIGHT, CATHY.

THEY'RE FIGHTING WITH INTELLIGENCE, IRVING. LOOK HOW MICHAEL TALKS TO HOPE... WITH INTEGRITY, HONESTY AND TOTAL, NON-SUPERFICIAL RESPECT FOR HER AS A HUMAN BEING. THIS IS HOW WOMEN WANT MEN TO BE!

ALSO, YOU HAVE TO LOOK LIKE THAT AND MAKE $300,000 A YEAR.

SCRAPE SCRAPE

SCRAPE SCRAPE CHIP HACK SHOVEL SCRAPE

COME ON... START! START, YOU UNGRATEFUL DUMPSTER!! START, YOU TRAITOROUS PILE OF CORRODED JUNK!! START!!!
sputter

ONCE AGAIN, I HAVE DUG BENEATH THE SURFACE TO DISCOVER SOMEONE I DON'T WANT TO KNOW.

WHY DON'T YOU CALL IRVING AND TELL HIM YOU WANT TO GO TO HIS PLACE WHEN HE'S FINISHED WITH WORK, NO MATTER WHAT TIME IT IS, CATHY?

I DON'T WANT TO GIVE HIM THE WRONG IMPRESSION.

IF IRVING CALLED AND ASKED YOU TO GO TO HIS PLACE, WOULD YOU GO, NO MATTER WHAT TIME IT WAS?
OF COURSE.

THEN WHY MAKE IRVING TORTURE HIMSELF TRYING TO FIGURE OUT A GRACEFUL WAY TO ASK IF IT'S SOMETHING YOU'RE PERFECTLY WILLING TO DO??

I DON'T WANT TO GIVE HIM THE WRONG IMPRESSION IF I CAN MAKE HIM PAY FOR IT.

I'VE HARDLY SEEN YOU AND ZENITH LATELY, ANDREA. WHERE IS SHE?
...HUH?... BABY IS SLEEPING. THE NICE BABY IS SLEEPING.

YOU LOOK WEIRD. ARE YOU OK?
YES. NICE MOMMY IS FINE. MOMMY IS ALWAYS FINE.

ANDREA, IT'S ME! CATHY! YOUR BUDDY!
AUNT CATHY IS NICE. DOES AUNT CATHY WANT JUICE?

DAY 242 OF TEETHING. DAY 243 WITHOUT A BABY SITTER.
GUISEWITE

CAN'T YOU GET A BABY SITTER AND GO OUT FOR ONE EVENING, ANDREA?
ZENITH IS SO CLOSE TO SAYING HER FIRST WORD, CATHY. WE COULDN'T LEAVE YET.

WE WERE HERE FOR HER FIRST SMILE, HER FIRST CRAWL, HER FIRST STEP... WE JUST CAN'T MISS THE MOMENT SHE SPEAKS HER FIRST LITTLE WORD.

NO!

NO NO! NO NO! NO NO! NO NO! NO NO!
CAN WE GO NOW?
NO.
GUISEWITE

BEFORE I LEAVE ZENITH WITH A BABY SITTER, I NEED TO GRADUALLY TEACH HER TO FEEL SECURE WHEN I'M NOT IN HER SIGHT, CATHY.

THIS IS CALLED "DISTAL COMMUNICATION"-- HI, ZENITH! MOMMY'S GOING TO THE KITCHEN! -- SHE'S CONSTANTLY REASSURED BY THE SOUND OF MY VOICE, MAKING IT POSSIBLE FOR ME TO ACTUALLY LEAVE A ROOM FOR UP TO....

I'M BACK! MOMMY'S BACK! MOMMY MISSED YOU! DID YOU DO ANYTHING CUTE WHILE MOMMY WAS GONE?!

...2.5 SECONDS. A WORLD RECORD.
GUISEWITE

ZENITH'S GROWING UP SO FAST, CATHY. LOOK AT HER. SHE CAN'T WAIT TO RUN OFF AND EXPLORE THINGS ON HER OWN.

SHE'S FEARLESS, CONFIDENT, DETERMINED... SHE HAS HER OWN IDEAS, HER OWN JOKES, HER OWN TASTES, HER OWN GAMES....

I THOUGHT YOU **WANTED** ZENITH TO BE INDEPENDENT.
OF COURSE I WANT HER TO BE INDEPENDENT.

I JUST DON'T WANT HER TO BE ABLE TO DO ANYTHING WITHOUT ME!!
GUISEWITE

I CAN CARRY ON AN INTELLIGENT CONVERSATION WHILE A TEETHING ONE-YEAR-OLD SHRIEKS IN MY EAR AND DROOLS DOWN MY NECK....

I CAN HEAR MY BABY'S EYES OPEN FROM FIVE ROOMS AWAY... I CAN COOK, CLEAN, WASH, SHOP, DO FREE-LANCE CONSULTING, AND THINK UP 300 NEW TODDLER ACTIVITIES PER MINUTE WHILE RECITING ITALIAN LULLABYES, ALL ON TWO HOURS OF SLEEP A NIGHT.....

I AM MOTHER! I AM INVINCIBLE!
YOU'RE PUTTING STRAINED BEETS IN THE COFFEE MAKER, ANDREA.

...AND I CAN MAKE CAPPUCCINO OUT OF STRAINED BEETS!!
GUISEWITE

ANDREA, WHY IS IT THAT WHEN OTHER PEOPLE'S BABIES RACE AROUND SCREAMING AND SMASHING THINGS THEY'RE "**UNCONTROLLABLE MANIACS**," BUT WHEN YOURS DOES IT, SHE'S "**DOING A PERFORMANCE ART PIECE ON CUTTING A MOLAR**"?

WHY IS IT THAT WHEN OTHER PEOPLE'S BOYFRIENDS CANCEL DATES TO WORK LATE EVERY NIGHT THEY'RE "**PARANOID NERDS, INCAPABLE OF FACING EMOTIONAL RISK**," BUT WHEN YOURS DOES IT, HE'S A "**DEVOTED PROFESSIONAL**"?

THE FINAL CEMENT OF FRIENDSHIP BETWEEN WOMEN....

...WE KNOW EACH OTHER TOO WELL TO SPEAK TO EACH OTHER ANYMORE.
GUISEWITE

WE BEGAN WITH A SIMPLE LITTLE VALENTINE IN THE FIRST GRADE...

OUR TASTES GREW UP. WE DREAMED OF FLOWERS, CANDY, CARDS, JEWELRY AND SULTRY LINGERIE....

TODAY, IN 1988, THE YEAR THE BABY BOOMERS SLAM FACE-FIRST INTO OUR 30s AND 40s, THE VALENTINE DESIRES OF THE MORE MATURE WOMAN HAVE FOUND AN EVEN MORE PASSIONATE VOICE....

RETIN-A !! I MUST HAVE RETIN-A !!
ANTI-WRINKLE SALVE DISCOVERED

PROBLEMS WITH IRVING AGAIN, CATHY ?

CHARLENE, PLEASE. A WOMAN IN MY STAGE OF LIFE DOES NOT TRY TO SOLVE BOYFRIEND PROBLEMS BY STUFFING HERSELF WITH PRE-VALENTINE CHOCOLATE.

I'M TRYING TO MAKE MY FACE BREAK OUT SO I CAN GO BEG FOR A PRESCRIPTION OF "RETIN-A."

HI. I'D LIKE AN IMMEDIATE APPOINTMENT WITH THE DERMATOLOGIST FOR TREATMENT OF MY, UM... ...BLEMISHES.
SORRY, THE DOCTOR IS BOOKED THROUGH JULY.

JULY ??

EVER SINCE THEY ANNOUNCED THAT "RETIN-A," A CREME PRESCRIBED FOR ACNE, HAS BEEN SHOWN TO REVERSE WRINKLES, WOMAN HAVE BEEN STAMPEDING OUR OFFICE.

HA, HA ! SOME WOMEN HAVE BEEN TOO EMBARRASSED TO ADMIT THAT'S WHY THEY WERE COMING, AND HAVE ACTUALLY TRIED TO DEVELOP CASES OF ACNE TO GET THE CREME !!

I THINK I SEE A COUPLE MORE WRINKLES, CATHY...
GET ME THE YELLOW PAGES, CHARLENE.

I GAINED FIVE POUNDS EATING CHOCOLATE SO MY FACE WOULD BREAK OUT SO I COULD GET A PRESCRIPTION FOR AN ACNE MEDICINE WHOSE SIDE EFFECT IS TO MAKE WRINKLES DISAPPEAR. THE DOCTORS WERE ALL BOOKED. I GOT 97 NEW GRAY HAIRS.

DESPERATE, I CHASED 14-YEAR-OLDS AT THE MALL AND OFFERED THEM $200 FOR THE CONTENTS OF THEIR PURSES, IN CASE THEY HAD TUBES OF ACNE CREME IN THEM.

NOW -- FAT, BROKE, WRINKLED, BLEMISHED, GRAY AND HUMILIATED -- I PREPARE FOR A ROMANTIC EVENING WITH A MAN WHO CASHED IN HIS I.R.A. TO BUY "MINOXIDIL", A HIGH-BLOOD-PRESSURE MEDICINE, WHICH HE POURS ON HIS HEAD IN A FRANTIC ATTEMPT TO POSTPONE BALDNESS.
SQUIRT!

IS IT JUST ME, OR HAS VALENTINE'S WEEK LOST A LITTLE OF ITS ZIP THIS YEAR?
GUISEWITE

WHAT'S IRVING PLANNING FOR VALENTINE'S DAY THIS YEAR, CATHY?
HARD TO KNOW, CHARLENE.
DIARY

IN 1985, HE WILLED HIMSELF TO GET THE STOMACH FLU... IN 1986, HE PSYCHED HIMSELF IN AN IMPACTED WISDOM TOOTH AND TOTAL AMNESIA....
DIARY

IN 1987, HE HAD THE FLU, AMNESIA, LARYNGITIS, SPRAINED WRISTS AND A MUSCLE SPASM IN HIS BACK THAT CREATED SUCH STRONG VIBRATIONS IN HIS ENERGY FIELD THAT ALL OF HIS APPLIANCES, INCLUDING HIS ENTIRE PHONE SYSTEM, SHUT DOWN.

EVERY YEAR HE FINDS A WAY TO GIVE MORE OF HIMSELF FOR VALENTINE'S DAY.
Guisewite

MY VALENTINE'S DAY RESOLUTIONS: I WILL GET OUT OF THIS RUT AND INTO A HEALTHY RELATIONSHIP!
I WILL QUIT DATING MEN WHO CAN'T COMMIT!

I WILL MEET NEW PEOPLE! GO NEW PLACES! DO NEW THINGS!
I WILL NEVER AGAIN GET PHYSICALLY CLOSE WITH SOMEONE WHO WON'T PUT MY NUMBER IN HIS AUTOMATIC DIALER!

CATHY?
DING DONG!
IRVING!!

... I WILL BROADEN MY CIRCLE OF WOMEN FRIENDS....
Guisewite

I HAVE TO WORK LATE TONIGHT, IRVING.
NO PROBLEM, HONEY. I UNDERSTAND.

OH, NO, YOU DON'T... IF YOU'RE UNDERSTANDING THE ONE TIME I HAVE TO WORK LATE, YOU'LL THINK I SHOULD BE UNDERSTANDING THE NEXT 300 TIMES YOU HAVE TO WORK LATE.

IT'S OK... I UNDERSTAND.

YOU ARE NOT GOING TO MANIPU-LATE ME WITH UN-DERSTANDING. HAH! I REJECT YOUR UNDERSTANDING!
YOU MAKE ME CRAZY, CATHY!

WHAT DID IRVING SAY ABOUT YOU WORKING LATE?
HE YELLED AT ME.
Guisewite

DID YOU GET TO THE DIGGS FIGURES YET, CATHY?
I HAD TO PUT THE DIGGS FIGURES ASIDE FOR THE SALEM REPORT.
RUSH

YOU FINISHED THE SALEM REPORT??
NO. THE SALEM REPORT GOT MOVED TO MAKE ROOM FOR THE MASSMAN EMERGENCY.

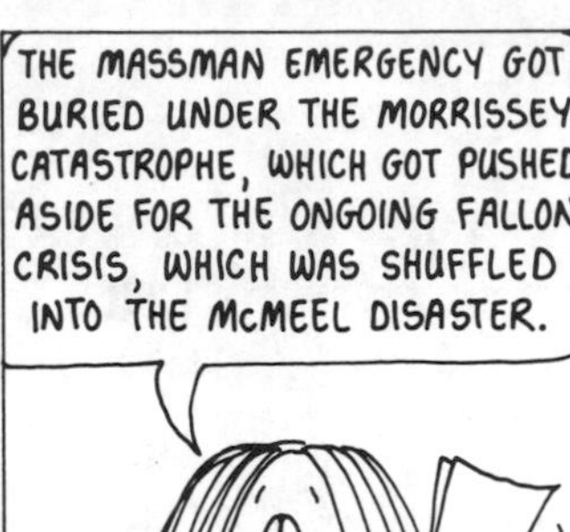
THE MASSMAN EMERGENCY GOT BURIED UNDER THE MORRISSEY CATASTROPHE, WHICH GOT PUSHED ASIDE FOR THE ONGOING FALLON CRISIS, WHICH WAS SHUFFLED INTO THE McMEEL DISASTER.

I ACCOMPLISHED NOTHING. IT TOOK ME ALL DAY JUST TO MAINTAIN THE MESS.
RUSH
GUISEWITE

I HAVE TO GO ON A BUSINESS TRIP TOMORROW, IRVING.
IF I SAY IT'S GREAT, SHE'LL THINK I DON'T CARE IF SHE'S HERE OR NOT.

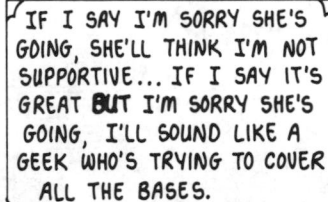

IF I SAY I'M SORRY SHE'S GOING, SHE'LL THINK I'M NOT SUPPORTIVE... IF I SAY IT'S GREAT BUT I'M SORRY SHE'S GOING, I'LL SOUND LIKE A GEEK WHO'S TRYING TO COVER ALL THE BASES.

IN TIMES LIKE THESE, A MAN HAS TO SUMMON HIS COURAGE AND DARE TO TRUST HIS MOST BASIC SURVIVAL INSTINCTS....

...PRETEND TO BE ASLEEP.
Z Z Z Z Z Z
GUISEWITE

WAIT, CHARLENE... I'LL GET TRIPLE BONUS POINTS IF YOU BOOK ME ON THIS AIRLINE, PLUS DOUBLE POINTS ON THIS OTHER AIRLINE IF YOU CHARGE IT ON THIS CHARGE CARD.

PLUS, I'LL GET TRIPLE POINTS ON THIS AIRLINE IF YOU BOOK ME WITH THIS RENTAL CAR COMPANY AND CHARGE IT ON THIS CARD, WITH ADDITIONAL GIFT POINTS WITH THIS HOTEL CHAIN IF I GET THE GAS WITH THIS CARD.

I'LL GET HOTEL POINTS AT THIS HOTEL, BUT IF TWO OF THE FLIGHT SEGMENTS ARE ON THIS AIRLINE, I'LL GET DOUBLE POINTS AT THIS HOTEL AND THIS RENTAL CAR COMPANY AND QUADRUPLE POINTS ON THIS CHARGE CARD PRIZE PROGRAM!!

NOW MORE THAN EVER, SUCCESS IS NOT A DESTINATION, IT'S A JOURNEY.
GUISEWITE

TWO BLOCKS FROM MY HOUSE TO THE CAR... HALF A MILE FROM THE CAR TO THE SHUTTLE BUS... FIVE MILES FROM THE BUS TO THE DEPARTURE GATE...
GATE 201
GATE

A QUARTER-MILE FROM THE GATE TO MY SEAT... THREE MILES FROM THE ARRIVAL GATE TO THE RENTAL CAR...
RENTAL CARS

400 YARDS FROM THE CAR TO THE MIDDLE OF THE LOBBY...
HERE, LET ME GET THAT FOR YOU.

YOU ONLY CARRIED IT TWO FEET !!
REGISTRATION
Guisewite

THAT'S ALL YOU'RE HAVING FOR DINNER, CATHY ?
YES. I'VE LEARNED TO KEEP IT LIGHT ON BUSINESS TRIPS, FRED.

A SALAD AND A GLASS OF PERRIER, AND I STAY MORE ALERT, AWAKE AND READY TO DO MY JOB.

GREAT. MAYBE YOU CAN REVISE THESE PROJECTIONS BEFORE OUR MEETING TOMORROW.
CERTAINLY! NO PROBLEM!

THIS IS ROOM 892. SEND UP A PLATTER OF BELGIAN WAFFLES AND A CHEESECAKE.
Guisewite

WRINKLE-FREE TRAVELING IN FOUR EASY STEPS:
STEP 1: CAREFULLY ROLL EACH GARMENT, FOLDING SLEEVES IN.

STEP 2: PLACE ROLLS IN SUITCASE BETWEEN LAYERS OF PLASTIC BAGS AND TISSUES.

STEP 3: LIFT CLOTHES FROM SUITCASE. GENTLY SHAKE.
STEP 4: IRON EVERYTHING.
Guisewite

THIS IS HOW IRVING MUST FEEL ON BUSINESS TRIPS...NO WONDER HE DOESN'T STAY IN BETTER TOUCH WHEN HE'S GONE.

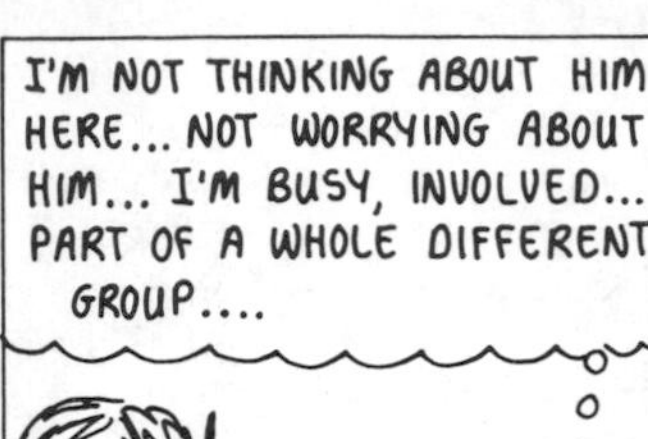
I'M NOT THINKING ABOUT HIM HERE... NOT WORRYING ABOUT HIM... I'M BUSY, INVOLVED... PART OF A WHOLE DIFFERENT GROUP....

HE'S NOT PART OF THE AGENDA ... NOT EVEN A FACTOR... HE'S TOTALLY OUT OF MY MIND!

SO, CATHY, WHAT'S YOUR ASSESSMENT OF BOB'S STRATEGY?
...HUH?

HOW MUCH LONGER IS OUR TAKEOFF DELAYED??
SHE JUST ANNOUNCED IT WOULD BE ANOTHER 45 MINUTES.

SHE SAID IT TO THE GROUP. SHE DIDN'T SAY IT SPECIFI-CALLY TO ME.
DO YOU ACTUALLY THINK THE FLIGHT ATTENDANT HAS TIME TO DISCUSS IT WITH EACH PASSENGER?

WELL, EXCUSE ME, BUT I PAID $89 FOR MY TICKET, AND I WANT A LITTLE INDIVIDUAL ATTENTION.
YOU ONLY PAID $89 FOR YOUR TICKET??

HOW MUCH LONGER IS OUR TAKEOFF DELAYED?!

SORRY. YOUR FLIGHT ARRIVED TOO LATE TO MAKE OUR LAST CONNECTION OUT TONIGHT.
I HAVE TO GET HOME!

I COULD RE-ROUTE YOU THROUGH CHICAGO, BUT YOU'LL HAVE FOUR STOPS, WITH TWO THREE-HOUR LAYOVERS.
ANYTHING! I HAVE TO GET HOME!! I HAVE TO GET HOME!!

...HOME!

I HAVE TO GET AWAY.

THEY RAVED ABOUT YOU IN ST. LOUIS, CATHY.
THANKS. YES. IT WENT VERY WELL.
VERY WELL? HA! YOU SAVED THE DAY! YOU CLINCHED THE DEAL!
THANKS. YES. THANK YOU SO MUCH.

BLEAH. BORING, IDIOTIC MEETINGS... DRONING DINNERS... THE WHOLE MISERABLE TRIP COULD HAVE BEEN HANDLED WITH ONE 10-MINUTE PHONE CALL! BLEAH!!

WHATEVER HAPPENED TO THE GOOD OLD DAYS WHEN SHE USED TO COME HOME AND TELL ME ABOUT DATES?

WHY DON'T I COME OVER THERE THIS EVENING, IRVING?
NO. YOU'VE BEEN TRAVELING, CATHY. I'LL COME THERE.

NO, REALLY. I DON'T MIND. I'D LIKE TO COME TO YOUR PLACE.
NO. I INSIST ON COMING THERE. PLEASE. I WANT TO DO THIS FOR YOU!

AACK!
VACUUM!
SCRUB!
DUMP!
STUFF!
WAD!
TRASH!
DUST!

...THERE. SEE? ISN'T IT NICE TO JUST HAVE A CHANCE TO RELAX?

TELL ME ALL ABOUT ST. LOUIS, CATHY!
WELL, I REALLY ONLY WENT BETWEEN THE AIRPORT AND THE HOTEL, MOM.

HOW DOES IT COMPARE WITH WASHINGTON?
IN WASHINGTON I JUST WENT BETWEEN THE AIRPORT AND THE CONVENTION CENTER.

DID YOU LIKE IT AS MUCH AS PITTSBURGH AND DENVER?
IN PITTSBURGH AND DENVER, I JUST WENT BETWEEN THE AIRPORT AND THE OFFICE BUILDINGS.

I'M FINALLY GETTING TO SEE THE WORLD, BUT IT KEEPS LOOKING LIKE THE INSIDE OF A TAXICAB.

I'LL NEVER MEET A MAN IN THIS STUPID TOWN, CATHY.
MY FRIENDS IN OTHER CITIES SAY IT'S JUST AS HARD THERE, CHARLENE.

HAH! I CHALLENGE ANY WOMAN TO COME TO THIS TOWN AND FIND A MAN WHO ISN'T MARRIED, GAY OR A TOTAL EGOMANIAC!
WELL, MY FRIENDS SAY...

THEY DON'T KNOW!! THIS IS AS BAD AS IT COULD GET!! PSYCHOTHERAPY HEAVEN! THIS IS ABSOLUTELY, POSITIVELY THE WORST POSSIBLE PLACE ON EARTH FOR A SINGLE WOMAN TO LIVE!!

FROM THE DEPTHS OF DESPAIR, A STRANGE NEW DAWNING OF CIVIC PRIDE...
Guisewite

I'M TOO OLD FOR THIS, CATHY.
SURE, WE'RE OLDER, CHARLENE, BUT THE MEN WE'LL MEET ARE OLDER, TOO.
SINGLE BUSINESS-PERSON MIXER

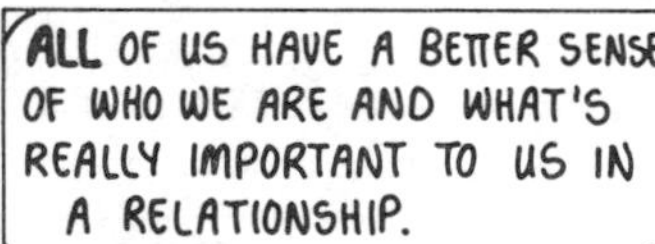
ALL OF US HAVE A BETTER SENSE OF WHO WE ARE AND WHAT'S REALLY IMPORTANT TO US IN A RELATIONSHIP.

SINGLE BUSINESS-PERSON MIXER

MEETING LATER IN LIFE GIVES A WOMAN A WONDERFUL ADVANTAGE WITH MEN!

WE DON'T HAVE TO GUESS WHICH ONES ARE GOING TO LOSE THEIR HAIR.
YOU'RE TOO YOUNG FOR THIS.
Guisewite

DATING... WHEW! IT'S HARD TO EVEN REMEMBER DATING!
YEAH, HA, HA! YOU HAVE TO PLAN A WEEK AHEAD TO GO OUT TO DINNER WITH YOUR HUSBAND!

THE IDEA OF BEING FREE JUST TO MEET SOME TOTAL STRANGER AND SPEND AN EVENING WITH HIM!
HA, HA! NO OBLIGATIONS! NO ROUTINES!!

IT SEEMS SO... ..SO TOTALLY REPULSIVE, CATHY.
OH.

FROM JEALOUSY TO NAUSEA... ...MY LIFE KEEPS EVOKING A DIFFERENT SHADE OF GREEN.
Guisewite

I THINK I LOOK GORGEOUS WHEN I'M STANDING IN THE LADIES' ROOM...THEN I GO OUT TO WHERE MY DATE IS AND I WANT TO RUN HOME AND CHANGE CLOTHES....

SOAP
SOAP

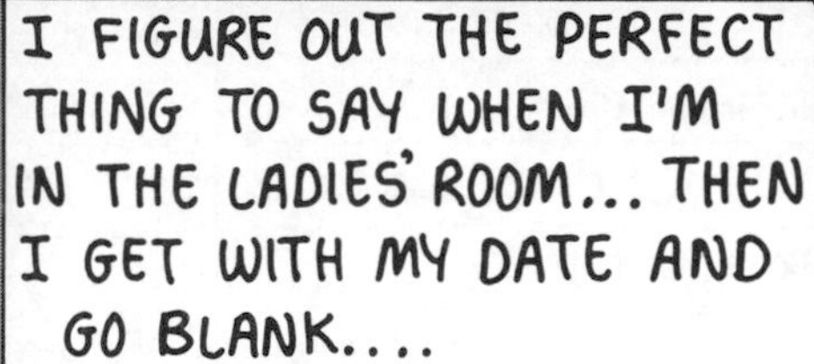
I FIGURE OUT THE PERFECT THING TO SAY WHEN I'M IN THE LADIES' ROOM... THEN I GET WITH MY DATE AND GO BLANK....

SOAP

IN THE LADIES' ROOM I'M CONFIDENT AND CHARMING... WITH MY DATE I'M A GEEK.
SOAP

WHERE SHOULD WE GO AFTER DINNER, CATHY ?
I WANT TO GO STAND NEAR A SOAP DISPENSER.

THE BALSAMIC VINEGAR IS EXPENSIVE, BUT IT'S GREAT.
OH...HELLO! ...AHEM... THANKS.
IF I'M TAKING THE TIME TO COOK, IT'S WORTH IT TO GET THE BEST!
YOU LIKE TO COOK??...ME TOO. HA, HA! SPARE NO EXPENSE!

YELLOWTAIL TUNA!
PEELED SHRIMP!
JAPANESE EGGPLANT!
OYSTER MUSHROOMS!
FRESH RASPBERRIES!
JAMAICAN BLUE MOUNTAIN COFFEE BEANS!

GOOD LUCK... ..UM.. MAYBE I'LL SEE YOU HERE AGAIN SOMETIME.
I'M SURE YOU WILL. I TRADE THE SHOPPING EVERY OTHER WEEK WITH MY BOYFRIEND!

MAY I HELP YOU?
YES. I'D LIKE TO RETURN THESE GROCERIES.
MANAGER
89¢

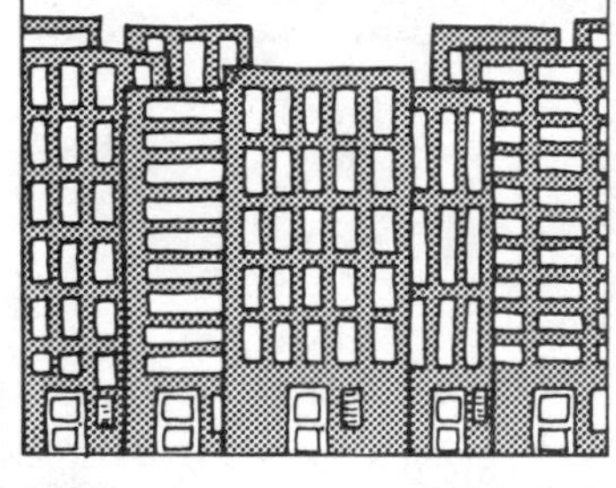
WHILE THEIR FRIENDS GOT ENGAGED, THEY GOT PROMOTED. WHILE THEIR FRIENDS TOOK LAMAZE CLASS AND MADE DINNER, THEY TOOK MEETINGS AND DID LUNCH.

SOME CALL THEM THE LOST GENERATION OF WOMEN. OTHERS SAY THEIR TIME HAS JUST NOW COME....

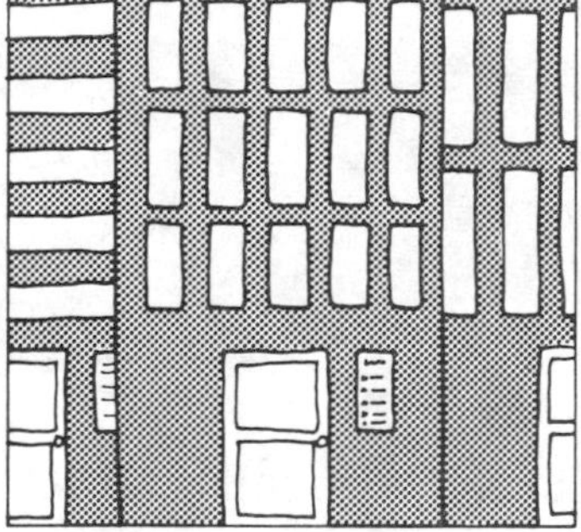

AFTER YEARS OF DEVOTING THEMSELVES TO DEVELOPING CAREERS, THE OVER-30 SET EMERGES THIS MARCH LIKE THE FIRST FLOWERS OF SPRING: BRAVE, CONFIDENT, PROUD, AND READY FOR LOVE.

THE DEBUTANTE CLASS OF 1988.
CLAIROL
RETIN-A
I ♥ LEAN CUISINE

MY 1975 LIST: HE MUST BE HANDSOME, STRONG AND CHARMING.

MY 1980 LIST: HE MUST BE HANDSOME, STRONG, CHARMING, OPEN, LOVING AND SUPPORTIVE.

MY 1985 LIST: HE MUST BE HANDSOME, STRONG, CHARMING, OPEN, LOVING, SUPPORTIVE, DYNAMIC, DEPENDABLE, SOLID, FLEXIBLE, POWERFUL, GENTLE, SERIOUS, SPONTANEOUS, SEXY, LOYAL, SOPHISTICATED, BOYISH, INDEPENDENT, DEVOTED, TOUGH, TENDER, BRILLIANT, HUMBLE, SUCCESSFUL, WISE AND CUTE.

MY 1988 LIST: HE MUST HAVE A SENSE OF HUMOR.

A WHOLE MONTH UNTIL TAXES ARE DUE... 11 WEEKS UNTIL I HAVE TO BE SEEN IN A BATHING SUIT... AND 47 DAYS UNTIL INVITATIONS START ARRIVING FOR THE SUMMER WEDDINGS OF THE ONLY DECENT REMAINING SINGLE MEN IN TOWN.

FOR A FEW INCREDIBLE WEEKS, THE CONCEPTS OF FINANCIAL SECURITY, PHYSICAL PERFECTION AND ROMANTIC BLISS ARE ALL STILL WITHIN MY GRASP!

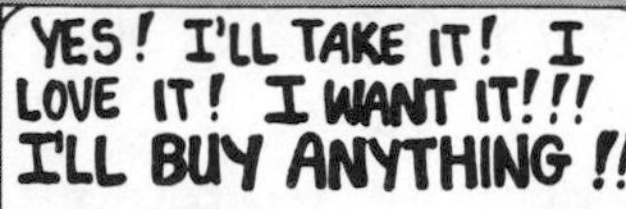
YES! I'LL TAKE IT! I LOVE IT! I WANT IT!!! I'LL BUY ANYTHING!!

NEW
NEW
NEW

THOSE WHO DREAM OF APRIL IN PARIS HAVE NEVER SEEN MARCH AT THE MALL.
NEW
NEW
Guisewite

FOR SPRING WE HAVE CLINGY LITTLE TOPS TO CELEBRATE THE NEW TREND IN CURVIER BUSTLINES...
Spring Fash

CROPPED JACKETS TO SHOW OFF THOSE FLAT TUMMIES... EENSY-BEANSY MINISKIRTS TO FLAUNT THOSE LEAN THIGHS AND NAUTILUS REARS...

AND, OF COURSE, YOU PULL IT ALL TOGETHER WITH THIS YEAR'S ALL-IMPORTANT NEW FASHION ACCESSORY...

THE PLASTIC SURGEON.
Spring f
Guisewite

THIS IS NICE.
IT'S 100% LINEN. YOU'LL HAVE TO IRON IT EVERY 15 SECONDS.
NEW!
LINEN

THE COLOR IS GREAT.
LIGHT PEACH. IT'LL GET FILTHY. YOU'LL SPEND A FORTUNE AT THE CLEANERS.

I REALLY LIKE IT.
IT'S TOO CASUAL FOR THE OFFICE, TOO TAILORED FOR A DATE. YOU'D BE THROWING PERFECTLY GOOD MONEY DOWN THE DRAIN!!

PERFECT! RING IT UP! I'LL TAKE IT!!
NOTHING MOVES THEM TO ACTION LIKE THE SOUND OF THEIR MOTHER'S VOICE.
Guisewite

LOOK. ISN'T THIS CUTE?
THIS BLOUSE COSTS $150.
SPRING

YES. ISN'T IT CUTE?
NO BLOUSE THAT COSTS $150 CAN BE CALLED "CUTE."

IT CAN BE "RAVISHING," "EXTRAORDINARY," EVEN "FANCIFUL"... BUT DO NOT FURTHER DISTORT THE ALREADY PATHETIC SCENE OF OVERPRICED WOMEN'S FASHIONS BY REFERRING TO A $150 SCRAP OF RAYON AS "CUTE"!!!

WOW, THAT'S REALLY CUTE, CATHY.
WRAP IT UP.
I NEED A VACATION.

THE HOTTEST NEW LOOK FOR SPRING IS STRIPES!
NO STRIPES.
STRIPES

STRIPES ARE FUN! STRIPES ARE FLIRTY!
I DO NOT WEAR STRIPES.
STRIPES

STRIPES ARE A WHOLE NEW WAY OF EXPRESSING WHAT WE ARE!!

FAT BEHIND BARS.
YOU SHOULDN'T WEAR STRIPES.

I THOUGHT YOU WEREN'T BUYING ANY NEW CLOTHES UNTIL YOU DEALT WITH WHAT YOU ALREADY HAVE.
I JUST DON'T HAVE TIME, MOM.

THERE ARE COMPANIES ALL OVER TOWN WHO'LL DO IT FOR YOU, CATHY... INSTALL SHELVES, BUILD IN LITTLE DRAWERS....

JUST CALL AND TELL THEM WHAT YOU NEED.

HELLO. I'D LIKE TO HAVE MY CLOSET BLOWN UP.

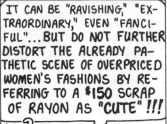

THE COLORS FOR SPRING ARE HOT, HIGH-VOLTAGE NEONS OR EARTHY BURNISHED METALLICS OR PRIMARY CHECKS AND DOTS OR FRILLY PASTEL FLORALS.
NEW

THE SKIRTS ARE LONG OR SHORT OR MEDIUM OR FULL OR DAINTY OR TRAMPY OR SLEEK... JACKETS ARE TINY AND TAILORED OR BIG AND BOXY OR SOFT AND SLOUCHY OR CLASSIC AND OFFICE-Y... PANTS ARE STRAIGHT OR BAGGY OR HALF-STRAIGHT, HALF-BAGGY OR TAPERED OR CROPPED OR STRETCHY OR HIGH-WAISTED OR LOW-WAISTED OR NORMAL-WAISTED OR WASHABLE SILK OR DRY-CLEANABLE RAYON OR ANY CONCEIVABLE THING IN BETWEEN.

IN SHORT, WE'VE TAKEN EVERYTHING THAT'S EVER BEEN FASHIONABLE AND THROWN IT OUT FOR GRABS, ALLOWING EACH CUSTOMER TO MAKE HER OWN FASHION STATEMENT!
NEW

AAACK!
EXCELLENT CHOICE. WE'RE SEEING A LOT OF THAT ONE THIS YEAR.
NEW

DID YOU SEE WHAT CATHY'S WEARING TODAY??
CATHY HAS SOMETHING NEW? I HAVE TO SEE!

WHAT IS IT? I WANT TO SEE!
NO, I HAVE TO SEE!
LET ME SEE!

I WANT TO SEE!
ME!
NO, ME!
ME!
ME!
ME!

THIS OFFICE GIVES NEW MEANING TO THE CONCEPT OF DRESSING FOR ONE'S PEER GROUP.

THIS CLOSET IS A CATASTROPHE, CATHY! YOU HAVE TO GET RID OF THIS STUFF!
THIS IS MY WARDROBE, MOM. I NEED EVERYTHING.

IT'S A DISASTER ZONE! YOU CAN'T LIVE LIKE THIS!
MOM, IT'S BEEN THIS WAY FOR A YEAR. IT'S NOT THAT BAD.

YOU'VE HUNTED THROUGH THIS MESS EVERY MORNING FOR A YEAR TO FIND SOMETHING TO WEAR??!

DON'T BE RIDICULOUS. THE CLOTHES I ACTUALLY WEAR ARE HEAPED ON THE CHAIR.

THE FIRST RULE OF CLOSET CLEANING: IF YOU HAVEN'T WORN IT IN TWO YEARS, IT'S OUT!
FINE. I HAVEN'T WORN THIS IN TWO YEARS. IT'S OUT!
OUT

THIS IS OUT??
I HAVEN'T WORN IT IN TWO YEARS.
YOU LOOK BEAUTIFUL IN THIS!
IT'S OUT OF STYLE, MOM. IT'S OUT!

WE COULD UPDATE IT WITH A NEW BELT...DYE IT A NEW COLOR...THIS IS THE DRESS YOU WORE ON MY BIRTHDAY IN 1983! YOU CAN'T THROW THIS SPECIAL DRESS OUT!!

THE SECOND RULE OF CLOSET CLEANING: DON'T DO IT WITH YOUR MOTHER.
OUT

I HATE CLEANING MY CLOSET, MOM.
I KNOW, CATHY... BUT IT'LL ALL BE WORTH IT WHEN YOU'RE DONE!
YES
NO
MAYBE

IMAGINE OPENING YOUR CLOSET AND SEEING ONE TIDY ROW OF CLOTHES THAT ALL FIT, ARE ALL IN STYLE, IN SEASON, CLEANED, MENDED, READY TO GO AND COLOR-COORDINATED WITH NEAT LITTLE PLASTIC BOXES FULL OF ACCESSORIES!!

WHEN WAS THE LAST TIME YOU HAD THAT EXPERIENCE, MOM?
IT'S LIKE SO MUCH IN THE LIFE OF A MOTHER, CATHY...

I WAS HOPING YOU COULD JUST DO IT AND TELL ME WHAT IT'S LIKE.
YES
NO
MAYBE

I WILL EAT BETTER FOOD.
CHOP! CHOP!

I WILL TAKE BETTER CARE OF MYSELF.... I WILL HAVE MORE ENERGY... I WILL UTILIZE MY POWER TO BE THE PERSON I WANT TO BE!!
CHOP! CHOP! CHOP! CHOP! CHOP! CHOP!

WHY DOES IT SEEM THAT WHEN A MAN TRANSFORMS HIS LIFE IT ALWAYS INVOLVES A BEAUTIFUL WOMAN...

...AND WHEN I DO IT, IT INVOLVES LITTLE CARTONS OF CRUNCHY VEGETABLES?

MAYBE I SHOULD GET THAT PINK BLOUSE...DO YOU THINK I SHOULD GET THE PINK BLOUSE, IRVING?
CATHY, YOU'VE BEEN TALKING ABOUT THAT PINK BLOUSE FOR THREE DAYS!

WHY YOU LIKE IT... WHY YOU NEED IT... HOW YOU'LL GET IT... WHAT YOU'LL DO WITH IT...

HOW COULD ONE PERSON SPEND SO MUCH TIME DWELLING ON ONE INSIGNIFICANT BLOUSE?!

THINK OF IT AS A FOOTBALL ON A HANGER.

THIS DRESS GOES OUT, CATHY. ICK. PITOOEE. DEFI-NITELY OUT!
I CAN'T THROW THAT OUT, MOM. I GOT IT ON SALE.
OUT
MAYBE

CATHY, IT'S UGLY, OUT OF STYLE AND TWO SIZES TOO SMALL.
I ONLY PAID $16.95 FOR IT.

$16.95? YOU'RE KIDDING!!
MARKED DOWN FROM $178!
DOWN FROM $178??!
IT WAS THE BUY OF MY LIFE!!
YOU CAN'T GET RID OF THIS!!
IT'S A TREASURE!

HOW ABOUT THIS NICE, NEUTRAL BLAZER?
I PAID A FORTUNE FOR IT. DUMP IT.
OUT
MAYBE

PANTS I HAVEN'T BEEN ABLE TO GET OVER MY KNEES SINCE THE EIGHTH GRADE... A DRESS I BOUGHT AS A WEIGHT-LOSS INCENTIVE IN 1977 THAT STILL HAS THE PRICE TAG ON IT...

A SKIRT I HAD ON FOR NINE SECONDS IN 1986 BEFORE THE ZIPPER EXPLODED...MISCELLANE-OUS JEANS AND TOPS THAT WOULD BE ADORABLE IF I HAD HEAD-TO-TOE LIPOSUCTION....

LIKE MILLIONS OF WOMEN, I EMERGE FROM MY SPRING CLEANING WITH A REALISTIC NEW SENSE OF WHO I AM...

...A CLOSET SIZE FIVE.
WHERE DO YOU WANT ME TO PUT THE CLOTHES THAT ACTUALLY FIT?

OH, GOOD. YOU'RE IN EARLY, CATHY. YOU CAN TAKE CARE OF THIS!
WAIT, I AL-READY...

OH, GOOD. YOU'RE IN EARLY, CATHY. YOU CAN HANDLE THIS!
OH, GOOD. YOU'RE IN EARLY, CATHY. YOU CAN DO THIS!
OH, GOOD. YOU'RE IN EARLY, CATHY. YOU CAN FIX ALL THIS!

IN SOME OFFICES, THE EARLY BIRD GETS THE WORM.

IN THIS OFFICE, THE EARLY BIRD GETS THE WORM, THE SLUGS, THE BEETLES, THE TOADS AND THE LIZARDS.

I'LL GET THE PHONE CALLS OUT OF THE WAY AND THEN I'LL BE ABLE TO THINK CLEARLY TO WRITE THE LETTERS...
CATHY

NO... I'LL WHIP OFF THE LETTERS, THEN I'LL BE ABLE TO ATTACK THE PHONE CALLS... ...NO... I'LL DO THE RESEARCH WHILE MY MIND IS FRESH AND THEN TACKLE THE PHONE CALLS AND LETTERS....
CATHY

... NO. I'LL GET THE READING OUT OF THE WAY AND THEN DO THE RESEARCH, LETTERS AND CALLS... NO! I'LL ALTERNATE...ONE LETTER...ONE CALL ... ONE READING...NO! I'LL CLEAN THE WHOLE DESK AND BEGIN THE RESEARCH...NO...

THE ENGINE IS RACING, BUT I CAN'T GET IT INTO A FORWARD GEAR.
CATH

I SPENT EVERY NIGHT LAST WEEK AND THE WHOLE WEEKEND CLEANING MY CLOSET... WHEW! WHAT A RELIEF THAT'S OVER!
OH, YEAH ... I SHOULD GO DO THAT, TOO.

NOW?? HAH! IRVING, YOU NEED BOXES, BAGS, LABELS, HANGERS, BELT RACKS, HOOKS, MENDING SUPPLIES....

YOU CAN'T START A MAJOR PROJECT LIKE THIS TEN MINUTES BEFORE WE GO TO THE MOVIES!
LET'S SEE.. ... THIS GOES OUT. BOOM. I'M DONE.

WHEW. WHAT A RELIEF THAT'S OVER!
YET ANOTHER REASON WHY MEN DESERVE ANY AMOUNT OF TORTURE WE CAN GIVE THEM IN LIFE.

WHAT DO YOU WANT, CATHY?
POPCORN IS LESS FATTENING, BUT FILLS UP MORE ROOM THAN A CANDY BAR...
SNACKS
POPCORN

IN THE LONG RUN, I'LL BE THINNER IF I EAT POPCORN, BUT IN THE SHORT RUN, IT WILL MAKE MY STOMACH STICK OUT MORE...
POPCOR

IF I HAVE THE CANDY BAR, MY WAIST WILL LOOK SLIMMER TONIGHT, BUT WILL BE FATTER BY FRIDAY....
POP

CATHY, THERE ARE 20 PEOPLE BEHIND US!! WHAT DO YOU WANT?!
I CAN'T ORDER UNTIL I KNOW WHETHER OR NOT I'LL BE SEEING YOU NEXT WEEKEND.
SNACKS
POPCORN

...TAXES?? AACK. I DON'T WANT TO HEAR ABOUT IT! I DON'T WANT TO THINK ABOUT IT! I DON'T WANT TO KNOW ABOUT IT!!

BLEAH! NOT NOW! NOT YET! NO! TAXES?? BLEAH! ICK ICK ICK!!
SLAM
BAM
BAM
BAM

CATHY, IT ISN'T THAT BAD... JUST CALL YOUR ACCOUNTANT AND MAKE AN APPOINTMENT.

THAT WAS MY ACCOUNTANT.
Guisewite

I CAN'T OPEN THE BOX. I CAN'T DO IT. I CAN'T FACE IT. I CAN'T LOOK. I DON'T WANT TO SEE.
1987 INCOME TAX STUFF

I'LL DO IT NEXT WEEK. NEXT MONTH. NOT NOW. I NEED TIME. I'LL GET AN EXTENSION. I'LL GO TO JAIL. WHO CARES. JAIL IS NICE. I HAVE TO LOOK. I HAVE TO OPEN THE BOX.
1987 INCOME TAX STUFF

I MUST OPEN THE BOX. I WILL OPEN THE BOX. I AM OPENING THE BOX!!

BRAVO.
WRONG BOX.
GIRL SCOUT COOKIES
1987 INCOME T STUFF
Guisewite

JAN. 1, 1987
EVERY EXPENSE RECORDED, EACH RECEIPT CROSS-REFERENCED TO A CATEGORY OF EXPENDITURE, PLOTTED ON A COMPUTER-GENERATED GRAPH AGAINST LAST YEAR'S COSTS.
JAN 1
JAN 1
JAN 1

JAN. 2 – DEC. 31, 1987
ALL RECORDS STUFFED IN A SHOPPING BAG THAT I SWORE I'D GET TO LATER.

24 PERFECT HOURS FOLLOWED BY 364 DAYS OF TOTAL DELUSION.

NEVER HAVE MY FINANCIAL LIFE AND MY LOVE LIFE BEEN SO TOTALLY IN SYNC.

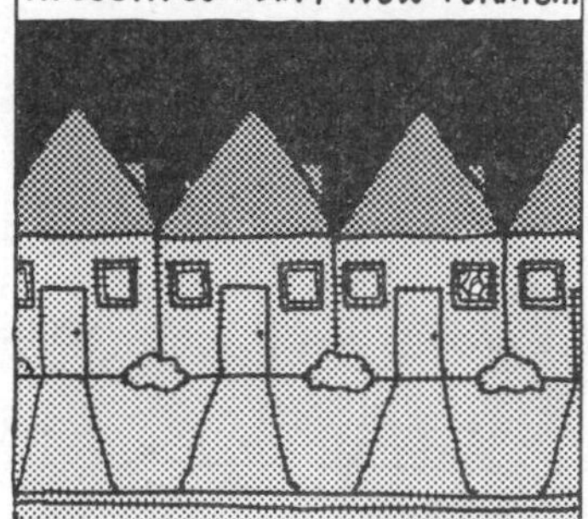
IT WILL BE KNOWN AS ONE OF THE MOST TRAUMATIC YEARS FOR INCOME TAX PREPARATION IN HISTORY. SO MANY NEW RULES... SO MANY NEW FORMS...

BUT IN THE LONELY QUIET OF NIGHT, IT ISN'T THE NEW TAX LAWS THAT WILL MAKE US SNAP, OR EVEN THE 24-HOUR BUSY SIGNAL AT THE IRS HELP HOTLINE...

WHAT WILL FINALLY SEND PEOPLE OVER THE EDGE IS FACING THAT MORE PERSONAL, POIGNANT AND UNLEGISLATABLE HORROR.....

I HAVE TOO MANY WRINKLES TO HAVE THIS LITTLE MONEY!!

THIS MAKES ME SICK, IRVING. LOOK AT THIS.
1987 RECEIPTS

JANUARY 4:
$241.00 FOR CLOTHES
JANUARY 19:
$86.22 FOR CLOTHES
FEBRUARY 13:
$104.66 FOR CLOTHES
MARCH 7:
$341.98 FOR CLOTHES
1987 RECEIPTS

MARCH 12:
$93.21 FOR CLOTHES
MARCH 14:
$113.74 FOR CLOTHES
APRIL 16:
$429.33 FOR CLOTHES
MAY 25:
$67.05 FOR CLOTHES
JUNE 6:
$527.48 FOR CLOTHES
JUNE 24:
$22.50 FOR CLOTHES

YOU'RE CRACKING, CATHY. LET'S TAKE A BREAK AND GO GET SOMETHING TO EAT.
I DON'T HAVE ANYTHING TO WEAR.

ENTIRE FAMILIES EARN A FRACTION OF WHAT YOU DO AND MANAGE TO SAVE MONEY EVERY MONTH... WOMEN WITH FIVE CHILDREN AND FULL-TIME JOBS MANAGE TO KEEP RECORDS BETTER ORGANIZED THAN YOU.
TAX STUFF 1987
MISC.

YOU ARE A DISGRACE. A SELF-INDULGENT EMBARRASSMENT! YOU SHOULD BE ASHAMED OF YOURSELF!

...OH YEAH?? PBLLLTT!!

IT'S HARD TO HAVE A MEANINGFUL DIALOGUE WITH YOURSELF AFTER 2 A.M.
TAX STUFF 1987
MISC.

MR. PINKLEY, WHO STAYED UP UNTIL 3 A.M., FINALLY HAS HIS TAX RETURN FINISHED, CHECKED AND READY TO SEND.
PRODU TESTII INC

CHARLENE, WHO STAYED UP UNTIL 2 A.M., HAS ALL HER TAX INFORMATION READY TO GIVE TO THE ACCOUNTANT.
1987
PRODU TESTII INC

CATHY, WHO CONVINCED HERSELF THAT IF SHE WENT TO BED AT 9:30 P.M., SHE'D GET UP EARLY AND DO EVERYTHING, AND THEN SMASHED OFF THE ALARM AND DIDN'T WAKE UP UNTIL 8:00,
PRODU TESTI INC

NOTHING IS AS EXHAUSTING AS GETTING ENOUGH SLEEP.
PRODU TESTI INC
Guisewite

"INCOME TAX FILING STATUS:"... SINGLE.

I WANT A SNACK.
NO SNACKS. I'M DOING MY TAXES.
I NEED TO GO SHOPPING.
NO SHOPPING!
I WANT TO RENT MOVIES.
NO MOVIES!
I HAVE TO WASH MY HAIR.
NO, NO, NO!

THERE WILL BE NO SNACKS NO SHOPPING NO MOVIES AND NO HAIR WASHING UNTIL I DO MY TAXES!!

"...NUMBER OF DEPENDENT CHILDREN:"... AT LEAST FOUR.
CHOCOLATE CHIP
HOT FUDGE
Chips
ICE CREAM
DONUTS
VHS
Guisewite

PLEASE TELL ME MY TAX RATE IS LOWER THIS YEAR.
YES. YOUR TAX RATE IS PROBABLY LOWER.
ACCOUNTANT

HOWEVER, BECAUSE OF THE COMPLEX NEW RULES, ACCOUNTANTS HAVE HAD TO TAKE HUNDREDS OF HOURS OF SPECIAL TRAINING AND SPEND MILLIONS REPROGRAMMING OUR COMPUTERS.

SO, WHILE YOU'LL PAY A FEW DOLLARS LESS IN TAX, WE HAVE TO CHARGE YOU TEN TIMES AS MUCH TO DO THE RETURN....
...WHICH IS THE GOVERNMENT'S LITTLE WAY OF GIVING TAXPAYERS THE ONE THING THEY'VE ALWAYS WANTED MOST...

...A VISIBLE TARGET.
ACCOUNTANT
Guisewite

I'M JUST NOT LOOKING TO GET INVOLVED RIGHT NOW.
ME EITHER. WHEW! NO BIG INVOLVEMENTS!
JUICE B
Work-out

I JUST BROKE UP WITH SOMEONE.
I'M TOO CONFUSED.
I'M TOO BUSY AT WORK.
I NEED TIME ALONE.
I HAVE NOTHING TO OFFER.
I'M JUST NOT READY.
I'M NOT INTERESTED.
I DON'T HAVE THE STRENGTH.

WOULD YOU LIKE LIKE TO GO OUT SOMETIME?
OK.

WHEN YOU'RE THIS FAMILIAR WITH THE PRODUCT, YOU QUIT PAYING ATTENTION TO THE DISCLAIMERS.

MORTGAGE INTEREST ON PEOPLE'S THIRD HOMES IS NO LONGER DEDUCTIBLE.
HA, HA! TOO BAD FOR THEM!
TAX SHELTERS ARE VIRTUALLY EXTINCT.
HA, HA! TOO BAD!
NEW TAX LAWS
TAX THERAPIST

HUGE BUSINESS ENTERTAINMENT DEDUCTIONS ARE GONE.
HOO, HA! SERVES THEM RIGHT!!
LONG-TERM CAPITAL-GAINS TAXES ARE SHOOTING UP.
HA, HA! TOO BAD FOR THEM!
NEW TAX LAWS

AND, OF COURSE, CHARGE CARD INTEREST IS ONLY 65% DEDUCTIBLE THIS YEAR AND ZILCH AFTER 1990.
NEW TAX LAWS
TAX THERAPIST
SPLAT.

I BELIEVE WE'VE FOUND THE RELEVANT PASSAGE.
NEW TAX LAWS
TAX THERAPIST
Guisewite

SINCE THE TAX REFORM ACT OF 1986, THERE HAVE BEEN 2,704 CHANGES IN THE INTERNAL REVENUE CODE, SENDING AN ALREADY BOGGLING STRUCTURE INTO TOTAL CHAOS.
IRS INFO.

IT MAKES ME SICK TO THINK MY HARD-EARNED MONEY IS JUST GOING TO GET LOST IN A SYSTEM THAT SPENT BILLIONS OF DOLLARS OVERCOMPLICATING ITSELF!
LOST?

NOT TO WORRY. YOUR ENTIRE 1987 TAX PAYMENT IS EARMARKED FOR REPRINTING OUR NEW FORM #8615: "COMPUTATION OF TAX FOR CHILDREN UNDER AGE 14 WHO EARN MORE THAN $1,000 A YEAR."
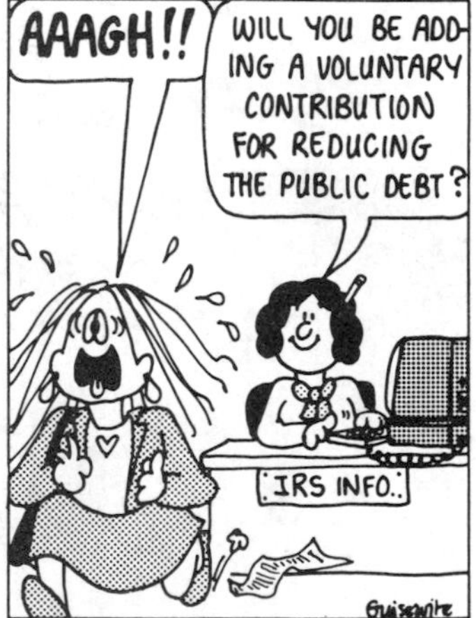
AAAGH!!
WILL YOU BE ADDING A VOLUNTARY CONTRIBUTION FOR REDUCING THE PUBLIC DEBT?
IRS INFO.
Guisewite

MY TAXES ARE IN. FINE. I'M BROKE. I'M IN DEBT. I'M IN A STATE OF FINANCIAL RUIN. BUT I AM NOT DEFEATED.

I WILL RISE ABOVE THE SHAMBLES. I WILL BEGIN ANEW!

I WILL ASTOUND THE WORLD WITH MY HEROIC DETERMINATION AND TRIUMPH OVER MY PAST!!

IT'S GOOD TO KNOW THAT 15 YEARS OF STARTING A NEW DIET EVERY MORNING HASN'T BEEN A TOTAL WASTE.
Guisewite

IRVING, YOUR OLD GIRLFRIEND IS AT THAT TABLE!
OH, YEAH... LET'S GO SAY HI.

SAY HI?? I CAN'T SAY HI TO YOUR EX-GIRLFRIEND WHEN I LOOK LIKE THIS! MY OUTFIT IS DISGUSTING! MY HAIR IS HORRIBLE!

CATHY, YOU LOOKED GOOD ENOUGH TO GO OUT WITH ME.
OF COURSE... HOW SILLY. I'LL JUST RUN TO THE LADIES ROOM FOR A SEC AND FRESHEN UP....

...AND SEE IF I CAN LOSE FIFTEEN POUNDS.
Guisewite

IRVING'S EX-GIRLFRIEND IS OUT THERE. I WILL NOT PANIC. I WILL NOT LOSE CONTROL.
EXIT
TOWELS
LADIES

IF I BELIEVE I'M CONFIDENT, I'LL COME ACROSS AS CONFIDENT... IF I BELIEVE I'M VIVACIOUS AND ATTRACTIVE, I'LL BE SEEN AS VIVACIOUS AND ATTRACTIVE!

I WILL MARCH INTO THAT ROOM KNOWING THE IMAGE I REALLY HAVE OF MYSELF IS THE IMAGE I WILL PROJECT!!

LADIES
Guisewite

WHY IS IT SO HARD TO SAY HELLO TO MY OLD GIRLFRIEND?
SHE'LL JUDGE ME, IRVING.

I HAVEN'T DATED HER IN YEARS. WHO CARES WHAT SHE THINKS?
I CARE WHAT SHE THINKS BECAUSE SHE USED TO CARE WHAT YOU THINK AND YOU MIGHT STILL CARE WHAT SHE THINKS.

CATHY, STOP WORRYING ABOUT WHAT EVERYONE THINKS FOR A MINUTE AND FOCUS ON THE ONE THING THAT REALLY MATTERS...

RIGHT. YOU'RE WITH ME NOW.
WHO'S THE GEEK?
Guisewite

CATHY, YOU REMEMBER MY EX-GIRLFRIEND, SHEILA?...SHEILA, REMEMBER CATHY?
OH, HI!
HI!

FLABBY ARMS
CHEAP DRESS
BAD NOSE JOB
SCRAWNY NECK
RIDICULOUS HAIR
HIDEOUS MAKEUP
FAT THIGHS
FLAT CHEST
TACKY JEWELRY
BUG EYES
NO WAIST
NAUSEATING COLOGNE.

PHONEY GRIN.

FINE. IRVING'S EX-GIRLFRIEND IS PRETTY, BUT I HAVE TALENT.
I JUST SOLD THE 98TH FRANCHISE OF THE LITTLE SHOP I OPENED!

FINE. SHE'S PRETTY AND TALENTED, BUT I HAVE CHARM!
THEY'RE PUTTING ME ON ALL THE TALK SHOWS! HA, HA! WHAT FUN!

FINE. SHE'S PRETTY, TALENTED AND CHARMING, BUT I HAVE IRVING!!
THIS IS MY FIANCÉ, STAN. WE'RE REMODELING A CHATEAU IN THE LOIRE VALLEY FOR OUR HONEYMOON!

TAKE ME HOME BEFORE I FIGURE OUT WHICH ONE OF US I HAVE TO KILL.

IRVING, IT HAD TO BOTHER YOU TO SEE YOUR EX-GIRLFRIEND WITH HER FIANCÉ.
WHY?...DID IT BOTHER YOU TO SEE A WOMAN I USED TO DATE BEING SO THRILLED WITH SOMEONE ELSE?

OF COURSE NOT. I'M VERY HAPPY WITH YOU.
ME, TOO. PERFECTLY HAPPY.
PERFECTLY HAPPY.
HAPPY AND FINE.
FINE.
FINE.

DON'T TOUCH ME!!

WHEN THINGS GET THIS HAPPY BETWEEN US, IT'S A GUARANTEED NO GOODNIGHT KISS.

ATTENTION ALL EMPLOYEES: THIS IS A TAPE RECORDING OF CHARLENE, YOUR ONE-WOMAN CLERICAL DEPARTMENT. GOOD MORNING AND WELCOME TO SECRETARIES WEEK.
IN

I DECIDED, WHAT BETTER WAY TO CELEBRATE THAN TO GO ON VACATION AND GIVE ALL OF YOU A CHANCE TO TAKE OVER MY DUTIES AND EXPERIENCE THE SECRETARIAL WORLD FOR YOURSELVES!
IN

I LEFT THE 9,700 "3-MINUTE PROJECTS" YOU GAVE ME TO DO ON FRIDAY AFTERNOON ON THE CORNER OF MY DESK.
IN

ASPIRIN, TUMS AND MY THERAPIST'S PHONE NUMBER ARE IN THE TOP DRAWER.
IN

WHERE'S THE TEMPORARY SECRETARY WE HIRED TO FILL IN FOR CHARLENE'S VACATION, CATHY?
SHE RAN OUT SCREAMING FOUR HOURS AGO.
OFF DUTY

WHERE'S THE BACKUP TEMP?
THE BACKUP TEMP THREATENED TO BLUDGEON THE MANAGEMENT SQUAD WITH HER ROLODEX AND HAD TO BE CARRIED AWAY.

IN TWO DAYS WE'VE DRIVEN 14 TEMPORARY SECRETARIES INSANE TRYING TO DO WHAT CHARLENE DOES EVERY DAY. IT SEEMS THAT SOME CHANGES ARE IN ORDER, DOESN'T IT?
I'LL SAY.

THERE WILL BE NO MORE VACATIONS FOR THE SECRETARIAL STAFF!!
WHEREVER YOU ARE, CHARLENE, KEEP GOING.

HOW COULD CHARLENE GO ON VACATION?! I HAVE A 300-PAGE REPORT TO REVISE TODAY!
I NEED THESE FAXED! DOES ANYONE KNOW HOW TO USE THE FAX??

CALL A MECHANIC! THE COPY MACHINE IS OUT OF PAPER!
WHERE'S THE GALANTE FILE? WHERE'S THE HOUSTON FILE? WHERE'S THE FILE CABINET?

WHERE'S CHARLENE? MY BIGGEST CLIENT IS STUCK ON HOLD!
WHERE'S CHARLENE? I NEED PLANE TICKETS!
WHERE'S CHARLENE?! THE COMPUTER IS ERASING ALL MY BILLINGS!!
HEE HEE HEE...

CHARLENE! I THOUGHT YOU WERE ON A TROPICAL ISLAND!
I DECIDED THE SCENERY HERE WOULD BE MORE MAJESTIC.

YOU'RE SPENDING YOUR VACATION HERE, TAKING SNAPSHOTS OF PEOPLE TRYING TO DO YOUR JOB, CHARLENE??
HEE, HEE... HERE'S TOM, "MR. PHONE CALL," TRYING TO WORK THE SWITCHBOARD....
CLICK!
RING RING RING BEEP BAM RING RING

HEE, HEE, HEE... HERE'S GRANT, WHO "DOESN'T NEED TO READ INSTRUCTIONS," DUMPING 870 HOURS OF FINANCIAL ENTRIES WITH ONE KEYSTROKE...
CLICK!

MR. PINKLEY, WHO REFUSED TO ATTEND MY 5-MINUTE COPIER DEMONSTRATION, COLLATING PART OF HIS OUTFIT WITH THE RUTLEDGE REPORT... HOO, HAH!!
CLICK!

...CHARLENE, BEING WELCOMED BACK FROM HER BRIEF BUT MEANINGFUL RESPITE...
CLICK!
Guisewite

YOU DO THE MENIAL DAY-TO-DAY WORK THAT ALLOWS THE REST OF US TO GET THE GLORY...
SECRETARIES WEEK

YOU ANTICIPATE EVERY NEED... COMFORT EVERY TROUBLE... WORK YOUR FINGERS TO THE BONE SUPPORTING OUR EFFORTS, AND STILL HAVE TIME FOR A CHEERY CUP OF COFFEE...

IN SHORT, WHILE WE CAN PAY YOU ONLY SECRETARIAL WAGES, YOU'RE MUCH MORE THAN A SECRETARY TO US, CHARLENE!
I KNOW. I'M A MOTHER.

OH, FOR HEAVEN'S SAKE.
YOU HAVE CREMORA ON YOUR NECKTIE.
SECRETARIES WEEK
Guisewite

YOU'RE AN EXCELLENT SECRETARY, CHARLENE. YOU HAVE OUR APPRECIATION.
I KNOW. BUT EVERYONE ELSE HAS THE WINDOW OFFICES AND COMPANY CARS.
SECRETARIES WEEK
YOU'RE PART OF THE TEAM!
I'M PART OF THE TEAM WHEN WE WORK UNTIL MIDNIGHT, BUT I'M OFF THE TEAM WHEN YOU HAND OUT THE BIG BONUS CHECKS.

IT'S TIME SECRETARIES STARTED GETTING THE RESPECT, PERKS AND JUMBO SALARIES OF THE EQUALLY INDISPENSABLE MEMBERS OF THE COMPANY!
WHAT WOULD YOU DO IF YOU SUDDENLY HAD ALL THAT?
ARE YOU KIDDING? HIRE A SECRETARY.
SECRETARIES WEEK
Guisewite

MEN JUST DON'T LET THEMSELVES BE VULNERABLE, GRANT.
ARE YOU KIDDING?

WHAT DO YOU THINK A MAN DOES EVERY TIME HE ASKS A WOMAN OUT FOR THE FIRST TIME, CHARLENE?

DO YOU HAVE ANY IDEA WHAT IT TAKES FOR A GUY TO LAY HIS WHOLE EGO ON THE LINE, RISK REJECTION ON EVERY LEVEL, WALK UP TO A WOMAN HE'S NEVER MET AND TRY TO ASK HER FOR A DATE?? HAH!!

PERFECT. THEY USE UP ALL THEIR VULNERABILITY BEFORE THEY GET TO KNOW US.

I'M GETTING WRINKLES WHERE MOM HAS WRINKLES... FAT WHERE MOM HAS FAT...QUIRKS LIKE MOM'S LITTLE QUIRKS...

THE THINGS MOM SAYS THAT DRIVE ME CRAZY ARE STARTING TO POP OUT OF MY OWN MOUTH..

I'M TURNING INTO MY MOTHER, CHARLENE!!
CATHY, YOUR MOM HAS SOME GREAT QUALITIES.

I KNOW...BUT I ONLY SEEM TO HAVE INHERITED THE ANNOYING ONES.
Guisewite

WHAT ARE YOU GIVING YOUR MOM FOR MOTHER'S DAY, ANDREA?
ZENITH DID THIS FABULOUS FINGER-PAINTING OF THE JOY SHE FELT THE FIRST TIME SHE MET GRANDMA. I'M HAVING IT FRAMED.

WHAT ARE YOU GIVING YOUR MOM FOR MOTHER'S DAY, TONY?
I'M SENDING A STRING QUARTET TO ANNOUNCE MY WIFE'S PREGNANCY. IT'LL BE MOM'S FIRST GRANDCHILD.
COFFEE ROOM RULES

WHAT ARE YOU GIVING YOUR MOM FOR MOTHER'S DAY, DIANE?
I'M GIVING HER A VIDEOTAPE LIBRARY OF MY SON SAYING, "I LOVE GRANDMA" IN 4 LANGUAGES.

SUDDENLY A BOTTLE OF COLOGNE SEEMS A LITTLE INSIGNIFICANT.
Guisewite

I'M IN THIS HORRIBLE PHASE WITH MY MOTHER, CHARLENE.
YEAH, ME TOO, CATHY.
CLEAN UP YOUR MESS

I LOVE HER...I NEED HER...I THINK ABOUT HER ALL THE TIME... BUT WHEN I'M FINALLY WITH HER, I'M DEFENSIVE, CRANKY AND IMPOSSIBLE TO BE WITH.
YEAH, ME TOO.

WHEN DID YOUR PHASE START?
BIRTH.
CLEAN UP YOUR MESS

ME TOO.
NO WONDER WE'RE SO GOOD AT IT.
Guisewite

TAKING YOUR MOM OUT IS A GREAT IDEA, CATHY.
THE ONLY TIME I SEE HER WE'RE IN ONE OF OUR KITCHENS. IT ISN'T HEALTHY.

IN MOM'S KITCHEN, I REVERT TO A 5-YEAR-OLD... IN MY KITCHEN, I FEEL I'M UNDER ATTACK...

FOR ONCE I WANT TO EXPERIENCE MY MOTHER WHEN WE'RE NOT SITTING IN SOMEONE'S KITCHEN !!
SO YOU'RE GOING TO A **RESTAURANT ??**
WE NEED TO BE **OUT** OF THE KITCHEN... I DIDN'T SAY WE WOULDN'T WANT TO BE **NEAR** ONE...

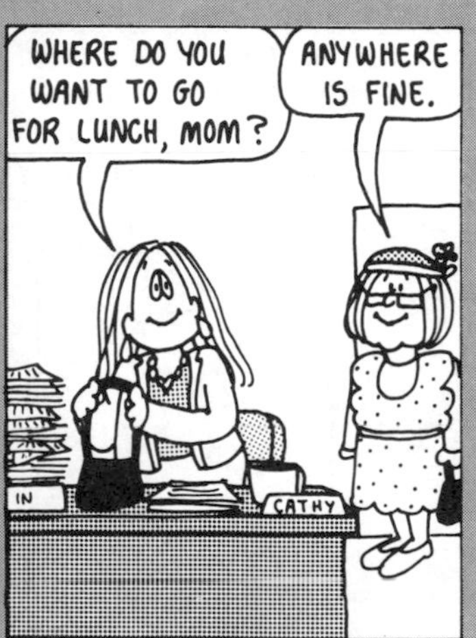
WHERE DO YOU WANT TO GO FOR LUNCH, MOM?
ANYWHERE IS FINE.
IN
CATHY

WHAT KIND OF FOOD DO YOU WANT?
ANYTHING.
WHAT DO YOU FEEL LIKE?
ANYTHING WOULD BE FINE.

MOM, JUST PICK SOMETHING!
SWEETIE, I'D SIT ON THE SIDEWALK AND EAT CRACKERS IF IT MEANT I COULD SPEND SOME TIME WITH YOU!

I DON'T KNOW WHICH IS **MORE** AGGRAVATING... THAT SHE REFUSES TO HAVE AN OPINION, OR THAT SHE'S QUOTING WHAT I SAID ON MY LAST DATE.

IF I ASK ABOUT IRVING, SHE'LL GET DEFENSIVE. IF I ASK ABOUT WORK, SHE'LL BE ANNOYED. IF I ASK ABOUT DIET, HOUSEKEEPING, GROOMING, FINANCES, BABIES, VITAMINS OR CORRESPONDENCE, SHE'LL GO CRAZY.

THERE ARE 133 SUBJECTS I ALREADY KNOW WILL TOTALLY AGGRAVATE HER.

...LEAVING ME WITH THE ONLY QUESTION A MOTHER REALLY EVER HAS LEFT...
DO I GO WITH A SURE THING OR TRY TO EXPAND MY REPERTOIRE?

SOMETIMES WHEN I LOOK AT HER I SEE MY OWN FACE.
MENU
MENU

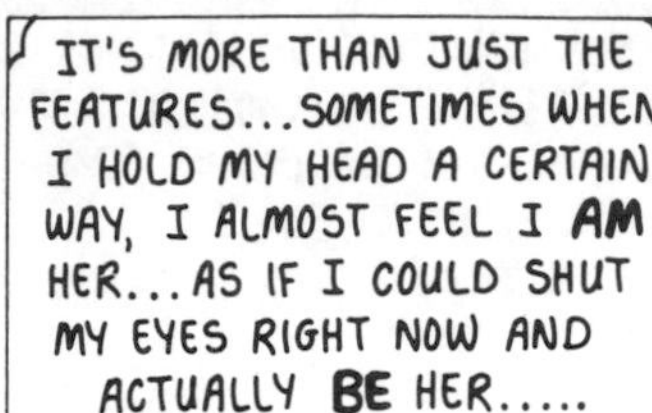
IT'S MORE THAN JUST THE FEATURES...SOMETIMES WHEN I HOLD MY HEAD A CERTAIN WAY, I ALMOST FEEL I **AM** HER...AS IF I COULD SHUT MY EYES RIGHT NOW AND ACTUALLY **BE** HER.....

MY BABY!
AACK! MY MOM!

...YET, INCREDIBLY, WE STILL MAINTAIN OUR OWN UNIQUE RESPONSES TO LIFE....
"PAT PAT PAT"
MENU
Guisewite

IF I EVEN MENTION YOUR LOVE LIFE, YOU LEAP TO THE CONCLUSION THAT I WON'T REST UNTIL YOU'RE MARRIED, CATHY.

IF I **DON'T** MENTION YOUR LOVE LIFE, YOU LEAP TO THE CONCLUSION THAT I'M AVOIDING IT ON PURPOSE BECAUSE DEEP DOWN I WON'T REST UNTIL YOU'RE MARRIED.
LADIES
TOWE

SWEETIE, I'M NOT **LIKE** THAT! WHY CAN'T YOU BELIEVE THAT AS LONG AS YOU'RE HAPPY, I COULDN'T CARE LESS IF YOU EVER GOT MARRIED??

THE BRIDE'S MAGAZINE STICKING OUT OF YOUR PURSE, MOTHER.
OK. FINE. SO WHO ARE YOU DATING?
SOAP
SOAP
Guisewite

THIS SALAD IS HUGE!
IT'S ONLY LETTUCE, MOM.
WELL, I'LL NEVER FINISH IT!
FINE. DON'T FINISH IT.

THEY SHOULDN'T SERVE SUCH HUGE PORTIONS.
SOME PEOPLE LIKE HUGE SALADS.
AND WHO COULD EAT ALL THESE ROLLS WITH A SALAD THIS BIG?
YOU DON'T HAVE TO EAT THE ROLLS.

IT'LL JUST GO TO **WASTE**! PERFECTLY GOOD FOOD GOING TO **WASTE**!!
MOM, IF THE RESTAURANT GAVE YOU A TEENY SALAD, YOU'D COMPLAIN THAT IT WAS TOO SMALL!!

DONE WITH YOUR SALADS?
HEAVENS, NO. WE'VE JUST FINISHED CHOOSING SIDES.
Guisewite

A WOMAN GETS TO AN AGE WHERE SHE FINALLY REALIZES HOW SILLY IT IS TO BE AT ODDS WITH HER OWN MOTHER.

I WANT TO HAVE YOU FOR MY FRIEND, MOM. THERE'S NO REASON WE CAN'T RELAX AND ENJOY A WONDERFUL, LOVING FRIENDSHIP!

THAT BUTTER'S GOING TO GO RIGHT TO YOUR THIGHS, DEAR.

AAUGH!!
SOMETIMES A MOTHER JUST HAS TO FEEL SHE CAN STILL MAKE AN IMPACT.
GUISEWITE

WANT TO ORDER A DESSERT, CATHY?

NO. **YOU** ORDER ONE, MOM. I'LL JUST HAVE A BITE OF YOURS.

NO. I ONLY WANT A BITE. **YOU** ORDER ONE AND I'LL HAVE A BITE OF YOURS.

I DON'T WANT A WHOLE ONE. I'LL JUST HAVE A BITE OF **YOURS.**

NO. YOU ORDER ONE.
YOU ORDER ONE.
YOU ORDER ONE.
YOU ORDER ONE.

DESSERT: THE CLASSIC RELATIONSHIP... EVERYONE WANTS ONE, BUT NO ONE WANTS TO CLAIM RESPONSIBILITY.
GUISEWITE

HOW WAS YOUR MOTHER-DAUGHTER LUNCH WITH CATHY?
I HAD THE TIME OF MY LIFE!!

YOU DIDN'T BUTT INTO THINGS THAT WERE NONE OF YOUR BUSINESS?
OH, YES! I BUTTED!
SHE DIDN'T SNAP AT YOU?
OH, YES! SHE SNAPPED!

YOU FOUGHT??
WE FOUGHT! WE ATTACKED! WE MADE EACH OTHER TOTALLY BERSERK... AND THEN WE PLOPPED DOWN TOGETHER AND SPLIT A CHEESECAKE!!

UNDERSTANDING ONE WOMAN IS TOUGH. UNDERSTANDING TWO OF THEM TOGETHER IS BEYOND COMPREHENSION.
GUISEWITE

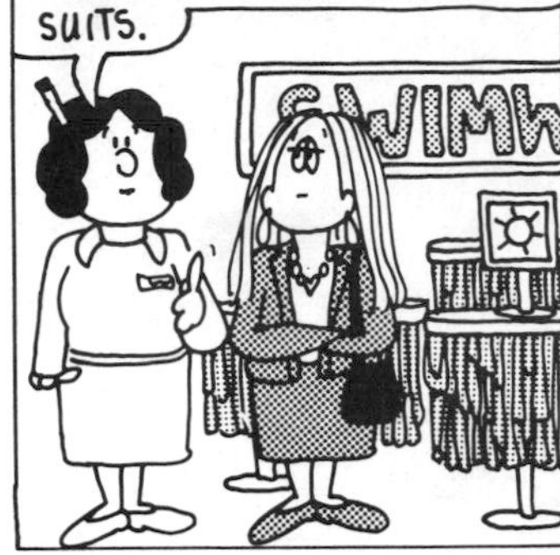
EVERY YEAR WOMEN RUN OUT OF THE BATHING SUIT DEPARTMENT SCREAMING THAT NO ONE COULD FIT INTO THESE SKIMPY SUITS.
SWIMW

ON BEHALF OF THE SWIMWEAR INDUSTRY, I WANT TO REASSURE YOU THAT THAT WILL NOT HAPPEN THIS YEAR.
YOU'VE DESIGNED MORE REASONABLE SUITS??

OH MY, NO! THIS YEAR WE HAVE **SWIMWEAR VIDEOS** SHOWING GORGEOUS MODELS ROMPING IN THE VERY SAME SKIMPY SUITS YOU SAID NO ONE COULD WEAR... PROVING ONCE AND FOR ALL THAT IT'S NOT **OUR** FAULT IF YOU LOOK LIKE A MARSHMALLOW IN THEM!!
VIDEO

AAUGH!!
WE MAY NOT COVER **THEIR** REAR ENDS, BUT AT LEAST WE'VE COVERED **OURS**.
VIDEO
Guisewite

THIS IS THE HOTTEST NEW THING IN SWIMWEAR...SEE? SNAP THE TOP TO THE BOTTOM AND ALL YOUR FAT WILL SQUISH OUT THE HOLE IN THE MIDDLE!
SWIMWEAR

UNSNAP THE TOP FROM THE BOTTOM, AND THE FAT CAN ROLL OVER THE WHOLE WAISTBAND!
SWIMWEAR

SNAP JUST **ONE** SIDE AND THE FAT WILL SQUISH OUT THE MIDDLE, ROLL OVER THE WAISTBAND **AND** BOINK OUT THE LEG HOLE! **THREE TOTALLY DIFFERENT LOOKS FOR JUST $65.99!**

...HELLO, MOTHER? WAKE ME UP WHEN IT'S WINTER.
Guisewite

AREN'T THE NEW SWIMSUITS FABULOUS? THEY SAY, "I'M FUN!"..."I'M FLIRTY!"..."I'M CONFIDENT!"... "I'M HIP!"... "I'M SPORTY!"..."I'M WILD!"...

MORE THAN EVER BEFORE, A SWIMSUIT REALLY SAYS SOMETHING ABOUT THE WOMAN WHO WEARS IT!!

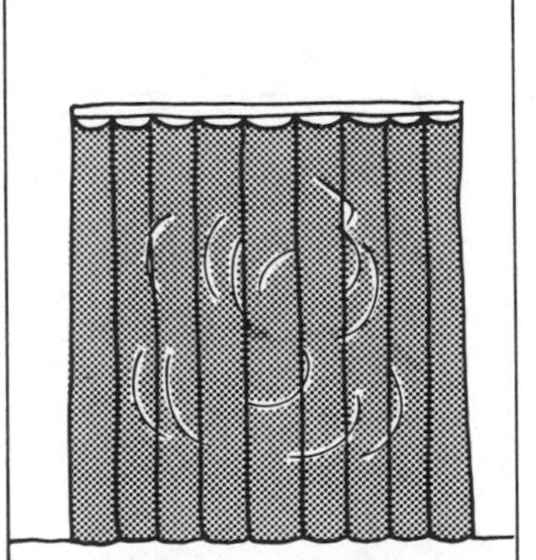

SHE HASN'T BEEN TO HER HEALTH CLUB IN 18 MONTHS!!
Guisewite

I'VE READ EVERY BOOK, STUDIED EVERY ARTICLE AND SIGNED UP FOR EVERY CLASS ON MALE PSYCHOLOGY, AND I STILL DON'T KNOW HOW TO REALLY REACH IRVING.

I'VE BEGGED FOR HINTS, PLEADED FOR CLUES...WHAT TO SAY... WHAT TO WEAR... HOW TO ACT..... ZILCH.

YET IRVING, WHO'S NEVER DONE ONE SECOND OF RESEARCH THE WHOLE TIME HE'S KNOWN ME, CAN GET TO ME WITH ONE TEENSY GLANCE.

HOW DO MEN ALWAYS KNOW WHERE THEY'RE GOING WITHOUT ASKING DIRECTIONS?

I AM A BEAUTIFUL PERSON. I HAVE MANY FINE QUALITIES.

I AM RESPECTED IN MY FIELD. I'M LOVED BY FAMILY AND FRIENDS. I AM SUCCESSFUL, BRIGHT AND CONFIDENT! I AM NOT AFRAID TO LOOK IN THE MIRROR!

I CAN LOOK. I AM PROUD OF WHO I AM! I AM NOT AFRAID TO LOOK. JUST TURN AND LOOK. SIMPLY TURN THE HEAD AND LOOK. SIMPLY UNLOCK THE NECK AND TURN THE HEAD....

DID YOU FIGURE OUT HOW TO GET THAT SWIM-SUIT ON?
YES. I JUST CAN'T FIGURE OUT HOW TO GET MY EYES OPEN.

HOW'S THAT BATHING SUIT WORK-ING OUT?
UM... I SORT OF LIKE IT, BUT I'M NOT SURE....

LET ME TAKE A PEEK!
A PEEK?? NO! NO PEEKING!! TOUCH THAT CUR-TAIN AND YOU'RE A DEAD WOMAN!!

THE ETERNAL BATHING SUIT DILEMMA...

I NEED SOMEONE TO TELL ME IT LOOKS OK, BUT I CAN'T STAND FOR ANYONE TO SEE ME IN IT.

OH, THIS ONE IS GROSS, CHARLENE. THIS IS HIDEOUS.
WELL, JUST TAKE IT OFF AND LET'S GO, CATHY.

THIS BATHING SUIT TAKES EVERY PART OF MY FIG-URE I HATE AND MAKES IT TEN TIMES WORSE!
FINE. LET'S JUST GO.
BOINK!
BOINK!

THIS IS BEYOND COMPREHENSION! THIS IS THE MOST REPULSIVE SIGHT I'VE EVER SEEN!!
CATHY, IF IT'S THAT BAD, WHY ARE YOU STILL STAR-ING AT IT?

I FEEL LIKE A SPECTATOR AT A TRAFFIC ACCIDENT.

FOR MILLIONS OF WOMEN, SHOPPING FOR A BATHING SUIT IS THE SINGLE MOST TRAUMATIC EVENT OF THE YEAR. IT'S USUALLY HUMILIATING, OFTEN HORRIFYING, AND ALWAYS HUMBLING...

YET EVERY YEAR WOMEN COME BACK TO TRY AGAIN. FOR MANY, IT'S A COURAGEOUS DISPLAY OF THE VERY QUALITIES THAT MADE THIS COUNTRY GREAT... THE SPIRIT TO TRY... THE NEED TO BELIEVE... THE BRAVE, BLIND HOPE THAT SOMEHOW, THIS YEAR WILL BE DIFFERENT....

EEYAACK!!

FOR OTHERS, IT'S DAY ONE OF AN AEROBIC EXERCISE PROGRAM

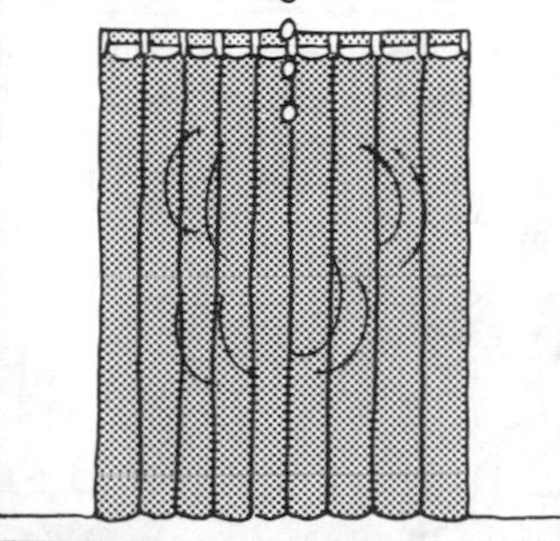
MAYBE IF I STUFF THE SHOULDER PADS FROM MY BLOUSE IN THE TOP OF THIS BATHING SUIT IT WOULD LOOK BETTER...

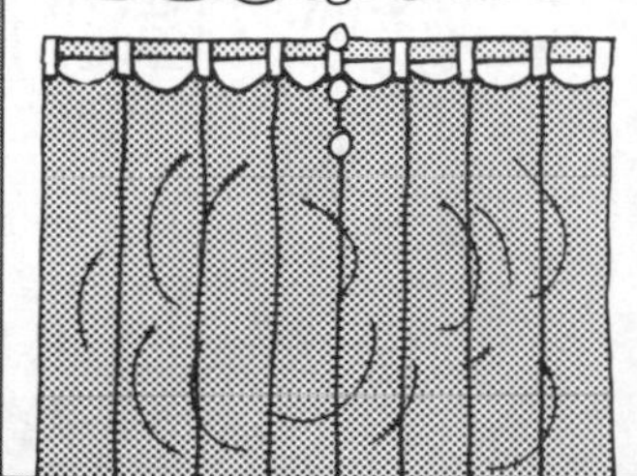
HEE, HEE... SHOULDER PADS IN THE TOP AND I'LL WEAR SUPPORT PANTYHOSE UNDER THE BOTTOM OF THE SUIT... HEE, HEE... WITH HIGH HEELS!... TA, DA! HA, HA!... TA.......

WARNING: THIS DRESSING ROOM IS MONITORED BY STORE PERSONNEL.

DID YOU NEED A DIFFERENT SIZE?
GO AWAY.

THE TOP HALF OF MY BODY AND THE BOTTOM HALF NEED TOTALLY DIFFERENT SIZES.
MANY WOMEN HAVE THAT PROBLEM.
SWIM WEAR

THAT'S WHY THE SIMPLE TANK SUIT HAS MADE SUCH A COMEBACK.

REALLY?

TANK SUIT

SEE? THE ONE PIECE OF SPANDEX FLATTENS THE CURVES AS IT SQUASHES THE BULGES, SO YOUR TOP AND BOTTOM WEIGHT GET SMOOSHED TOGETHER EVENLY TO CREATE ONE HULKING FORM IN THE SHAPE OF A MILITARY TANK!
TANK SUITS

YOU'RE GOING TO TRY IT ON??

IT'S BETTER TO BE ONE TANK THAN TWO OF WHAT I RESEMBLE WHEN I PUT ON A BIKINI.

HOW DID THE SIZE 14 WORK OUT?
I WANT TO KNOW WHY THEY BOTHERED TO MAKE THIS BATHING SUIT LARGER THAN A SIZE 2.

DID SOMEONE THINK A SIZE 14 BODY COULD ACTUALLY LOOK GOOD IN A SUIT LIKE THIS??

DO THE PEOPLE WHO DESIGN SUITS KNOW WHAT BEING A SIZE 14 USUALLY INCLUDES ON THE FEMALE FORM?!
I BOUGHT THIS IN A SIZE 14 FOR MYSELF AND IT LOOKS JUST ADORABLE, THANK YOU.

OH.
I SEWED UP THE SIDES AND USE IT FOR A LITTLE COIN PURSE.

BATHING SUIT #1:
THE WOMAN IS WILLING TO TOTALLY TRANSFORM HERSELF TO MAKE THE RELATIONSHIP WORK.

I'LL LOSE WEIGHT! I'LL EXERCISE! I'LL HAVE LIPOSUCTION!

BATHING SUIT #2:
THE WOMAN TRIES TO TRANSFORM THE OTHER PARTY TO MAKE THE RELATIONSHIP WORK.

MAYBE IT WILL STRETCH.. MAYBE I CAN ADD AN EXTRA PANEL...

BATHING SUIT #3:
THE WOMAN REJECTS THE WHOLE RELATIONSHIP BEFORE EVEN SAYING HELLO.

BLEAH. NOT MY TYPE.

BATHING SUITS #4-#50:
THE WOMAN RE-PLEDGES HERSELF TO THE JOYS OF REMAINING UNINVOLVED.

WHICH WAY TO THE MUUMUU DEPARTMENT?!

CATHY, WHAT'S WRONG?
I JUST SPENT ANOTHER THREE HOURS TRYING ON BATHING SUITS, IRVING.

COME HERE... YOU NEED A HUG.
AACK! DON'T TOUCH ME! I FEEL OBESE! I FEEL LIKE A BLIMP!!

HOW AM I SUPPOSED TO BE LOVING AND SUPPORTIVE IF YOU WON'T LET ME NEAR YOU?

COMFORT ME FROM ACROSS THE ROOM!!

I THOUGHT I HEARD IRVING SAY HE'D SEE YOU LATER, CATHY.
NOT EXACT-LY...
CORN

WHEN IRVING SAYS HE'LL SEE ME LATER, IT MEANS HE'LL CALL NEXT WEEK... IF HE SAYS HE'LL **TALK** TO ME LATER, IT MEANS HE'LL SEE ME IN A DAY OR TWO.

POPCORN

IF HE JUST SAYS "BYE," IT MEANS I'LL ACTUALLY BOTH SEE HIM **AND** TALK TO HIM LATER.
YOU HAVE TO MEET SOMEONE ELSE, CATHY.

I COULDN'T LEAVE HIM NOW, CHARLENE. I'VE JUST DECIPHERED HIS CODE.

IT'LL BE LONG HOURS AND GRUELING WORK, BUT WHOEVER TAKES THIS PROJECT ON COULD BE IN FOR A BIG PROMOTION!

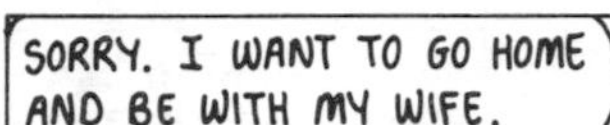
SORRY. I WANT TO GO HOME AND BE WITH MY WIFE.

SORRY. I WANT TO GO HOME AND BE WITH MY KIDS.
SORRY. I WANT TO GO HOME AND BE WITH MY HUSBAND AND BABY.

TA DA! LOOKS LIKE IT'S UP TO YOU, CATHY!

I WANT TO GO HOME AND BE WITH MY ANSWERING MACHINE.

WHAT'S THAT SOUND?? IT'S 9:00 AT NIGHT. EVERYONE WENT HOME HOURS AGO. THERE SHOULDN'T BE ANY SOUNDS.
CATHY

...SOMEONE'S BROKEN INTO THE OFFICE AND IS GOING TO MURDER ME. I'M GOING TO BE MURDERED IN THIS STUPID OFFICE. MURDERED BECAUSE OF THE STUPID WEXNER PRESENTATION. IT'S GETTING CLOSER. I CAN'T MOVE. I'M PARALYZED AND NOW I'M ABOUT TO BE MURDERED....

DO YOU HAVE ANY-THING FOR A HEADACHE IN HERE?
YEAAAK!

THANKS. VERY EFFEC-TIVE. ANYTHING FOR A STOMACHACHE?

MY NAME'S MITCH. I STAYED LATE TO WORK ON A PRESENTATION.
OH... SORRY I CRUSHED YOU WITH THE DESK. I THOUGHT YOU WERE A MURDERER.

WHY DO WOMEN ALWAYS ASSUME ANY MAN IN THE OFFICE AT NIGHT IS A MURDERER?
SORRY. WHY DON'T WE FINISH THE PRESENTATION TOGETHER AND WE CAN BOTH GET OUT OF HERE?

TOGETHER? HAH! I HARDLY THINK YOU COULD HELP ME ON THE WEXNER PRESENTATION!!
THE WEXNER PRESENTATION IS MY ACCOUNT!

OH. SORRY. I THOUGHT YOU WERE THE CLEANING LADY.
POINK!

WHEW! I'M BEAT. WANT TO STOP SOMEWHERE FOR A DRINK, CATHY?
A DRINK?

DOES HE MEAN "DRINK," AS IN "POTENTIAL DATE"...OR "DRINK," AS IN "FRIENDLY CO-WORKER DRINK"?

"DRINK," AS IN "START A SERIES OF PERSONAL COMPLICATIONS THAT WILL DESTROY MY CAREER"... OR "DRINK," AS IN "DEVELOP THE KIND OF GREAT BUSINESS FRIENDSHIP THAT COULD HELP SHOOT ME TO THE TOP"??

WHAT DO YOU SAY?
I DIDN'T UNDERSTAND THE QUESTION.

HA, HA! I CAN'T BELIEVE WE'VE BEEN TALKING FOR TWO HOURS, MITCH!
HA, HA! ME EITHER! YOU'RE GREAT, CATHY!
YOU'D BETTER LET YOUR WIFE KNOW YOU'RE RUNNING LATE!
HA, HA! I'M NOT MARRIED! BUT CALL YOUR HUSBAND IF YOU WANT!

OH, I'M NOT MARRIED.
YOU'RE NOT MARRIED?
NO. YOU'RE LIVING WITH SOMEONE, THOUGH, AREN'T YOU?
NO. YOU?
NO.
OH.

OH... AHEM...
HEH... UH....

NOTHING KILLS THE CONVERSATION LIKE DISCOVERING EVERYONE AT THE TABLE IS AVAILABLE.

"A PERSON WHO'S BEEN DATING MORE THAN TEN YEARS APPROACHES ROMANCE WITH UNDERSTANDABLE NEW CAUTION."
PSYCHOLOGY

"AT THIS POINT IN HER DATING CAREER, HEARTS HAVE BEEN TRAMPLED, EXPECTATIONS SHATTERED, FEELINGS TRASHED, AND HOPES SQUASHED LIKE LITTLE MARSHMALLOW VALENTINES."
PSYCHOLOGY

"AS SHE TEETERS ON THE BRINK OF YET ANOTHER INVOLVEMENT, SHE'S GUIDED BY THE MATURE VOICE OF SELF-PRESERVATION."
LEAP! YES! GO FOR IT!!

YOU SHOULD HAVE SEEN ME BEFORE.
PSYCHOLOGY

WANT TO GET SOME LUNCH, CATHY ?
UM, I'D BETTER NOT, MITCH. PEOPLE IN THE OFFICE MIGHT START TALKING.

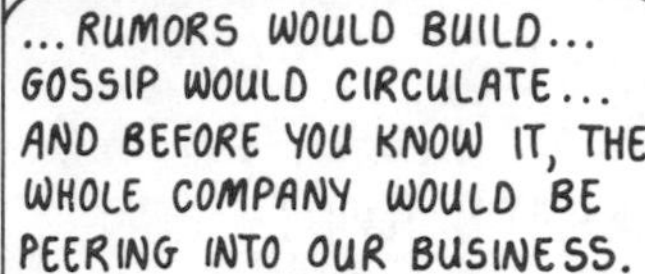
...RUMORS WOULD BUILD... GOSSIP WOULD CIRCULATE... AND BEFORE YOU KNOW IT, THE WHOLE COMPANY WOULD BE PEERING INTO OUR BUSINESS.

WANT TO ORDER IN ?
Guisewite

WELL, DON'T YOU LOOK NICE TODAY IN YOUR **BRAND-NEW OUTFIT,** CATHY ???
I'VE WORN THIS BEFORE, CHARLENE.

YOU DIDN'T RUN OUT AND BUY A **BRAND-NEW OUTFIT** IN CASE YOU RUN INTO YOUR **BRAND-NEW LOVE INTEREST** IN THE HALL ??
I HAVE WORN THIS DOZENS OF TIMES. YOU JUST NEVER NOTICED.

HI, CATHY.
OH... MITCH! AHEM... UM...HI!
AMAZING HOW WELL THOSE PRICE TAGS HOLD UP THROUGH SO MANY WASHINGS.

AACK !!
WELL, DON'T YOU SMELL NICE TODAY IN YOUR **BRAND-NEW COLOGNE,** MITCH ???
Guisewite

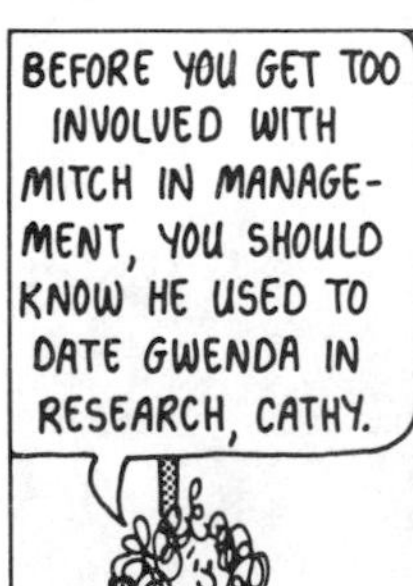
BEFORE YOU GET TOO INVOLVED WITH MITCH IN MANAGEMENT, YOU SHOULD KNOW HE USED TO DATE GWENDA IN RESEARCH, CATHY.
OH, NO. IT'S BAD ENOUGH TO DATE SOMEONE FROM THE OFFICE...

...BUT IF HE'S ALREADY DATED SOMEONE **ELSE** IN THIS **SAME** OFFICE, IT'S **HORRIBLE! WHO DOES HE THINK I AM??** ONE OF HIS "GIRLS"?? JUST ANOTHER CHEAP OFFICE CONQUEST?

OH, CHARLENE, YOU'RE A WONDERFUL FRIEND FOR LETTING ME KNOW! HOW DID YOU EVER FIND OUT ??!

I TOLD HIM HOW YOU USED TO DATE GRANT IN ACCOUNT SERVICES.
AH.
Guisewite

I WILL NOT TELL MY MOTHER I MET SOMEONE NEW. IT'S WAY TOO EARLY. I WILL NOT MENTION IT. NOT A PEEP.

I WON'T EVEN TALK TO MOM. I DON'T WANT TO BE TEMPTED. I'LL JUST SAY HELLO TO DAD. JUST A QUICK HI TO DAD...

HELLO?
I'M DATING SOMEONE NEW FROM THE OFFICE, DAD! HANDSOME, FUNNY, TALENTED, BLOND, 5'11" I'M SO EXCITED!!

...UM, DON'T TELL, MOM, THOUGH, OK?
YEAH, RIGHT...

I KNOW YOU'VE WORKED LATE A LOT, BUT I WAS HOPING YOU AND MITCH COULD GO OVER THESE...

.....MITCH?? WITH MITCH?? ...AHEM.. WELL, YES. I COULD STAY A BIT... YES! AHEM... NO PROBLEM! CONSIDER IT DONE!!

HI, MITCH... IT LOOKS AS IF WE HAVE A BIG NIGHT AHEAD OF US!
OH, I CAN'T STAY LATE TONIGHT, CATHY.

NEED ANYTHING BEFORE I GO HOME, CATHY?
BRING ME A ROLL OF MASKING TAPE AND WRAP IT AROUND MY MOUTH.

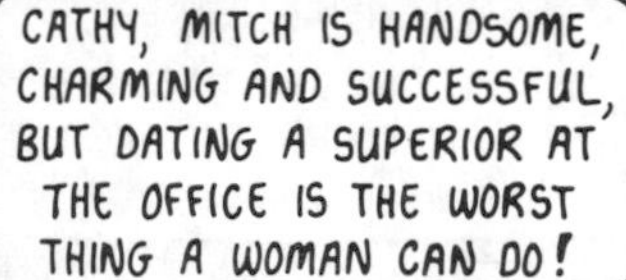
CATHY, MITCH IS HANDSOME, CHARMING AND SUCCESSFUL, BUT DATING A SUPERIOR AT THE OFFICE IS THE WORST THING A WOMAN CAN DO!

COFFEE ROOM RULES

NOT ONLY WILL YOU FLING YOUR PERSONAL LIFE OUT FOR INSPECTION BY EVERYONE IN OUR COMPANY... BUT YOU'LL NEVER BE ABLE TO GET ANOTHER PROMOTION WITHOUT EVERYONE WONDERING WHY!

AND WHAT IF YOU AND MITCH BROKE UP??... WHAT DO YOU THINK WOULD HAPPEN THEN??

...I'D ASK HIM OUT.
COFFEE ROOM RULES

WAITER, THE ICE IS MAKING MY PERRIER GO FLAT!
UH, OH. HE'S THE LOUD, OBNOXIOUS TYPE IN RES- TAURANTS. DON'T GET INVOLVED.

OOPS. YOU DIDN'T WANT ANY ROLLS, DID YOU?
LOUD AND SELFISH. BIG TROUBLE.
I THINK I WAS POISONED BY THE APPETIZER.
LOUD, SELF- ISH AND A HYPOCHON- DRIAC.

ALL THE WARNING SIGNS ARE THERE. THE FLAGS ARE UP. CALL IT QUITS. CALL IT OFF. BAIL OUT NOW WHILE YOU HAVE A CHANCE....

THERE'S NOTHING WORSE THAN KNOWING A RELATION- SHIP IS DOOMED BEFORE THE ENTRÉE ARRIVES.
Guisewite

ATTENTION ALL EMPLOYEES: IN THE CONTINUING SAGA OF OUR LATEST OFFICE ROMANCE, CATHY AND MITCH WERE LAST CITED IN A SECRET RENDEZVOUS AT THE ARUGULA CAFE LOOKING...
RECEPTION

CHARLENE, MITCH AND I DID **NOT** HAVE A GOOD DATE LAST NIGHT... WE WILL **NOT** BE DAT- ING IN THE FUTURE... WE MAY NOT EVEN BE **SPEAKING** TO EACH OTHER, SO YOU CAN JUST SHUT DOWN YOUR GOSSIP FACTORY ONCE AND FOR ALL!

ATTENTION ALL EMPLOYEES: THE FUN HAS JUST BEGUN!
RECEPTION
Guisewite

INFATUATED, SHE SEARCHES THE HALLS FOR HIM, SENDING OUT PSYCHIC MESSAGES.
WHERE ARE YOU?? WHERE ARE YOU??

...LATER, ATTEMPTING TO BREAK UP, SHE TRIES DESPER- ATELY TO AVOID HIM.
DON'T LOOK. DON'T LOOK. DON'T LOOK. DON'T LOOK.

OH, HI, CATHY!
AACK.

LIFE IN THE OFFICE: BY THE TIME THE MESSAGE GETS PICKED UP, THE PROJECT HAS BEEN CANCELED.
WHY WHY WHY WHY...
Guisewite

NO. WE CANNOT GO OUT TO DINNER ANYMORE.

CATHY, DISCUSSING BREAKING UP OVER FOOD DOES NOT COUNT AS "GOING OUT TO DINNER."

AS SOON AS WE'RE OUT OF THE OFFICE, IT MIGHT SEEM LIKE A DATE.

I KNOW IT'S NOT A DATE. YOU KNOW IT'S NOT A DATE. WHO'S GOING TO THINK IT'S A DATE??

"HOW I LOST THE WEIGHT"... ..."100 POUNDS OFF IN 100 DAYS!"..."MY MIRACLE WEIGHT LOSS PLAN"..."EAT YOUR WAY TO A SIZE 5".....
DIET
MY Miracle Diet

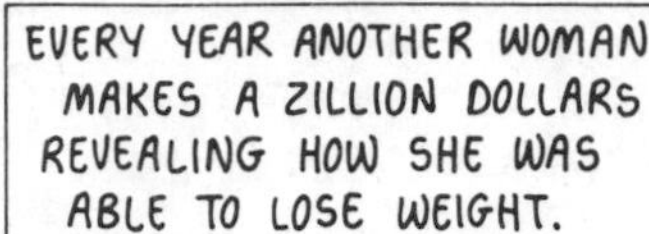
EVERY YEAR ANOTHER WOMAN MAKES A ZILLION DOLLARS REVEALING HOW SHE WAS ABLE TO LOSE WEIGHT.

THE BITTERSWEET REALIZATION OF EVERY DIETER....
NEW
NEW

I MAY BE CARRYING A FEW EXTRA POUNDS, BUT I'M SITTING ON A BEST SELLER.
diet soda
CATHY
Guisewite

HOW'S YOUR NEW DIET, CATHY?
GREAT! AHEM... HA, HA... I WAS JUST, UM, SEEING IF I LEFT MY STAPLER IN THE REFRIGERATOR.

AREN'T YOU ON A NEW DIET, CATHY?
YES...AHEM...THIS IS **SOY CAKE**. **DIETETIC SOY CAKE**. THIS IS **ALLOWED** ON THE DIET.
IN

HOW'S THAT NEW DIET, CATHY?
THE DIET IS **FINE**. **THE DIET IS GOING EXACTLY ACCORDING TO SCHEDULE!!!**

I KEEP LOSING FACE... THE ONE PART OF MY BODY THAT ISN'T OVERWEIGHT.
Guisewite

THIS IS A BUSINESS MEAL. THE CALORIES DO NOT COUNT.

I AM MENTALLY LABELING THESE AS "BUSINESS CALORIES" SO MY BODY WILL KNOW THEY WERE EATEN IN THE LINE OF DUTY AND WILL PROCESS THEM DIFFERENTLY.

DO YOU HEAR THAT, BODY?? UNDER **NO** CIRCUMSTANCES AM I TO BE PUNISHED FOR ITALIAN FOOD I ATE WHILE BEING BORED TO DEATH BY THIS CLIENT! FLAG THESE CALORIES PAST! NO TOLL! NO FAT!

...CATHY??
SORRY. I WAS JUST GOING OVER THE TORTELLINI DEAL.

TO BE ATTRACTIVE TO MEN THIS SEASON, WOMEN ARE SPENDING THEIR LIFE SAVINGS TO BE KNOCKED UNCONSCIOUS AND HAVE FAT SURGICALLY SUCTIONED OFF THEIR KNEES AND REARS SO THEY CAN CRAM THEMSELVES INTO $200 MINISKIRTS.
LIFE
SPORTS

TO BE ATTRACTIVE TO WOMEN THIS SEASON, MEN ARE BUYING A CAN OF MOUSSE AND A PAIR OF SUSPENDERS.
LIFE
SPORTS

SPORTS

NOTHING WE EVER DO IS GOOD ENOUGH.
LIFE
Guisewite

I WILL NOT EAT A SNACK JUST BECAUSE I'M WATCHING TELEVISION.

I HAD A NICE DINNER TWO HOURS AGO. I DO NOT NEED A SNACK. I DO NOT EVEN WANT A SNACK.

I MAY NOT EVEN THINK ABOUT GETTING UP FROM THIS CHAIR AND GETTING A SNACK!!!

...SO MUCH FOR RELAXING IN FRONT OF THE TV SET.

GINGERED SEA URCHIN PATÊ WITH LEMON GRASS?
NO, THANKS... I'M WATCHING MY WEIGHT.

BLACKENED "MAHI" WITH CARAMBOLA AND CARDOON?
CILANTRO-BASTED CRAWFISH ON AMARANTH CAKES?
NO, THANKS... I'M WATCHING MY WEIGHT.

...CATHY, HOW COULD YOU PASS UP ALL THAT GREAT FOOD AND THEN COME HOME AND EAT CHOCOLATE CHIP ICE CREAM?!

IF IT'S GOING TO BE WITH ME FOR THE NEXT FIVE YEARS, I WANT IT TO BE SOMEONE I KNOW.

DO I WEIGH MYSELF OR NOT? DO I RISK RUINING MY WHOLE DAY... DO I TAKE THE CHANCE?

I HAVE TO KNOW. NO MATTER WHAT THE OUTCOME, IT'S BETTER TO BEGIN THE DAY WITH A FIRM GRIP ON THE TRUTH!!

MY SCALE IS INACCURATE.

MOM! WHAT ARE YOU DOING HERE DRESSED LIKE THAT??
FLO NEKERVIS AND I HAVE GONE INTO BUSINESS AS PERSONAL TRAINERS.

AFTER SPENDING OUR LIVES TELLING OUR CHILDREN TO EAT RIGHT AND GET ENOUGH EXERCISE, WE ARE **NOT** GOING TO SIT THERE WHILE YOU THROW YOUR MONEY DOWN THE DRAIN ON SOME "PROFESSIONAL" WHO'LL JUST TELL YOU THE SAME THING!!

YOU WANT A MOTHER?? YOU **HAVE** A MOTHER!!!

GET OUT OF MY HOUSE!
EXCELLENT. NOTHING GETS THE CIRCULATION GOING LIKE A BRISK JOG.

FLO AND I CAN'T STAND THAT OUR CHILDREN ARE HIRING OTHER PEOPLE TO FORCE THEM TO DO WHAT WE'VE BEEN BEGGING YOU TO DO YOUR WHOLE LIVES.

YOU HIRE THE DIET COUNSELOR, FITNESS TRAINER, CLOSET ORGANIZER, FINANCIAL ADVISER, RELAXATION EXPERT... WHAT DO YOU THINK THESE GENIUSES ARE GOING TO TELL YOU, CATHY??

EAT YOUR VEGETABLES!
GET SOME EXERCISE!
HANG UP YOUR CLOTHES!
SAVE YOUR MONEY!
GO TO BED AT A DECENT HOUR!

HELLO? I'D LIKE TO MAKE AN APPOINTMENT WITH THE THERAPIST.

READY FOR TOE TOUCHES? ..AND **ONE** AND **TWO** AND...
SHE'S NOT DOING THE TOE TOUCHES, ANNE.

MOM AND FLO... NO OFFENSE, BUT MOST PERSONAL TRAINERS DEVOTE YEARS TO PERFECTING THEIR OWN PHYSIQUES BEFORE THEY TRY TO INSTRUCT OTHERS.

I MEAN, LOOK AT YOU... WHAT KIND OF INSPIRATION DO YOU THINK YOU OFFER??

THIS IS WHAT WILL HAPPEN TO YOU IF YOU DON'T FOLLOW OUR PROGRAM.
...AND ONE AND TWO AND....

I'M STARVING ON THIS DIET YOU AND FLO WORKED OUT FOR ME, MOM.
WE'RE ON THE DIET, TOO, CATHY. WE'RE ALL STARVING.
BODY

WE'RE STARVING... WE'RE CRANKY... BUT WE'LL MAKE IT! WE HAVE THE WILL! WE HAVE THE STAMINA! WE HAVE THE PANACHE!
BODY BY FLO & ANNE
BODY BY FLO & ANNE

BODY BY FLO & ANNE
BODY BY FLO & ANNE

NEXT TIME, TRY ENDING YOUR SPEECH WITH A WORD THAT DOESN'T SOUND SO MUCH LIKE "PANCAKE."
HOUSE OF PANCAKES
BODY
BODY BY FLO

I'VE BEEN ON YOUR PROGRAM FOR A WEEK AND I'VE GAINED 3 POUNDS, MOM.
WEIGHT DOESN'T MATTER, CATHY. ALL THAT COUNTS IS INCHES!
BODY BY FLO & ANNE
BODY BY FLO & ANNE

I'VE GAINED AN INCH IN MY WAIST.
INCHES AND WEIGHT DON'T MATTER. WHAT COUNTS IS HOW YOUR CLOTHES FIT!
BODY BY FLO & ANNE
BODY BY FLO & ANNE

I CAN'T GET MY "FAT" JEANS ZIPPED.
CLOTHES, INCHES AND WEIGHT DON'T MATTER. WHAT COUNTS IS THAT YOU'VE SPENT SPECIAL TIME WITH YOUR MOTHER THAT YOU'LL TREASURE THE REST OF YOUR DAYS!!
BODY

...SALESWOMANSHIP!
WHAT DO WE SAY WHEN WE GET A CLIENT WE'RE NOT RELATED TO?
BODY BY FLO & ANNE
BODY BY FLO & ANNE

HOW DOES DAD FEEL ABOUT YOUR NEW CAREER AS A PERSONAL TRAINER, MOM?
BODY

OH, IT'S REALLY OPENED HIM UP, CATHY!

ANY INTIMIDATION HE MAY FEEL BECAUSE OF MY NEW PROFESSIONAL ASSURANCE AND POLISH IS MORE THAN COUNTERED BY THE NEW EXCITEMENT AND VIBRANCY I BRING TO OUR RELATIONSHIP!!
BODY BY FLO ANNE
BODY BY FLO & ANNE

WHERE'S MY DINNER??
I'D BETTER GET HOME BEFORE MY HUSBAND OPENS UP.

ZENITH, MOMMY AND DADDY LOVE YOU MORE THAN ANY-THING IN THE WORLD, BUT WE NEED TO TAKE A LITTLE VACA-TION WITHOUT YOU.
COUNTRY INNS

WE'LL THINK ABOUT YOU EVERY MINUTE AND CALL YOU EVERY DAY AND BRING YOU LOTS OF PRESENTS... BUT IT'S IM-PORTANT FOR DADDY AND ME TO SPEND A LITTLE TIME JUST WITH EACH OTHER!!

OH, LUKE... MAYBE YOU CAN SAY IT BETTER....

MOMMY AND DADDY ARE GOING ON A GUILT TRIP.

I'M HAPPY TO WATCH ZENITH WHILE YOU'RE GONE, ANDREA, BUT WHAT'S WRONG WITH YOUR NORMAL SITTER?
ABAB!
YES, SWEETIE, MOMMY WILL GET YOU SOME PEACH YOGURT!

GOOBLM!
YES! YOU CAN EAT IT WHILE YOU WATCH THE "MacNEIL-LEHRER NEWSHOUR"!
BAKGAP!
OF COURSE YOU CAN WEAR YOUR FLUFFY YELLOW SLIPPERS!

OUR REGULAR SITTER WILL BE HERE ON THE WEEKDAYS, BUT THE ONLY ONE I COULD GET FOR THE WEEKEND BARELY SPEAKS ENGLISH, CATHY.

I'M JUST AFRAID SHE WON'T UNDER-STAND WHAT ZENITH WANTS.
PLOKM!
BANANA? FLASH-LIGHT? DATSUN? VOLLEY-BALL?

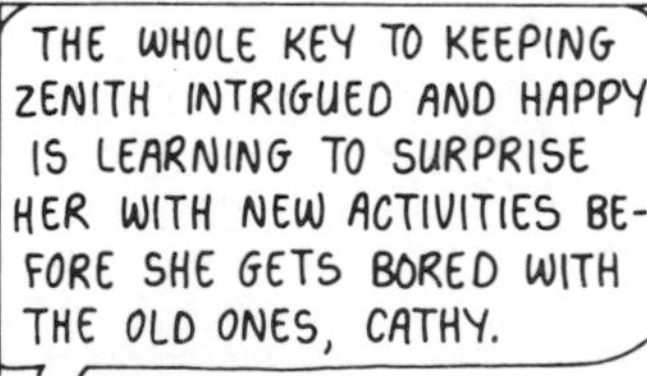
THE WHOLE KEY TO KEEPING ZENITH INTRIGUED AND HAPPY IS LEARNING TO SURPRISE HER WITH NEW ACTIVITIES BE-FORE SHE GETS BORED WITH THE OLD ONES, CATHY.

BAM BAM
BAM BAM

IT'S SIMPLE HUMAN PSYCHOLOGY, REALLY...
BABY BOOK

STOP AN ACTIVITY BEFORE SHE'S REALLY READY TO STOP AND SHE'LL ALWAYS BE EAGER FOR MORE AND EXCITED ABOUT HER NEXT SESSION WITH YOU!
RIP RIP RIP
RIP RIP
JUICE

ALL SET TO TAKE CARE OF ZENITH, CATHY?
NO, BUT I'M MORE PREPARED FOR MY NEXT DATE.
SPLAT
SPLAT
SPLAT
SPLAT

HERE, CATHY, YOU'LL NEED ZENITH'S CAR SEAT... DIAPERS... HAT... BIBS... BOTTLES... CLOTHES... PUZZLES... BLANKET... BEAR... BOOKS... SING-ALONG TAPES... TOWELS...

JUICE... CHEERIOS... CRACKERS... BANANAS... SQUASH... APPLESAUCE... SPOONS... YOGURT... DINOSAURS... FLASH CARDS... LEGOS... TRAIN SET... BUSY BOX... POP BEADS... AND CRAYONS.

THAT SHOULD HOLD US FOR THE WEEKEND, ANDREA.
LEGO

THE WEEKEND?? THAT'S FOR THE CAR RIDE TO YOUR HOUSE.
LEGO

HERE ARE PHONE NUMBERS FOR OUR HOTEL, THE POLICE DEPARTMENT, THE FIRE DEPARTMENT, THE HOSPITAL, OUR DOCTORS, OUR RELATIVES, THE FBI AND THE SWAT TEAM.

HERE'S A FIRST-AID KIT, CPR TRAINING FILM, POISON ANTIDOTE CHART, SNAKEBITE KIT, BABY MEDICAL LIBRARY, AND INSTRUCTIONS IN CASE OF FIRE, EARTHQUAKE, FLOOD, TIDAL WAVE, TORNADO, HURRICANE, TYPHOON OR LOCUST INVASION.

ANYTHING TO ADD, ANDREA?
SNAKE BITE KIT
CPR
FIRST AID
Baby Medicine
Baby Medicine II

CANCEL THE STUPID VACATION AND GIVE ME BACK MY BABY!!
WE DON'T GET OUT MUCH.

ANDREA AND I ARE GOING TO A REMOTE COUNTRY INN. NO PHONE... NO TV... JUST A QUIET, HUMBLE PLACE WHERE WE CAN REDISCOVER EACH OTHER.
COUNTRY INNS

OF COURSE, WE'RE TAKING OUR CELLULAR PHONE AND ANSWERING MACHINE SO YOU CAN CALL US ABOUT THE BABY.
AND WE'RE TAKING OUR PORTABLE TV AND STEREO IN CASE THERE'S A DISASTER THAT COULD AFFECT THE BABY.

AND WE'RE TAKING OUR VCR, 48 TAPES, A GELATO MAKER AND AN ESPRESSO MACHINE IN CASE... IN CASE.....
COUNTRY INNS

IN CASE WE WANT TO STAY UP ALL NIGHT REVIEWING SUITABLE FUTURE MOVIES FOR THE BABY!!
RIGHT. IT'S FOR THE BABY.

MY EX-WIFE AND I HAVE TWO CHILD-REN.
NO. TOO GUILT-RIDDEN. I'D NEVER GET IN-VOLVED WITH A MAN WHO HAS CHILDREN.

I'VE NEV-ER HAD CHILDREN, BUT I WAS MARRIED ONCE.
NO. TOO DISILLU-SIONED. I'D NEV-ER GET INVOLVED WITH A MAN WHO'S BEEN DIVORCED.

I'VE NEV-ER BEEN MARRIED AND NEV-ER HAD CHILDREN.
NO. UNSTABLE AND NEUROTIC. I'D NEVER GET INVOLVED WITH A MAN WHO CAN'T COMMIT.

WHY CAN'T WE MEET THE KIND OF MEN WE WANT TO DATE, CATHY?
AND WHO HAS ANY IDEA WHAT KIND THAT WOULD BE?
OPEN
Guisewite